IN THE SHADOW OF THE BEAR

IN THE SHADOW OF THE BEAR

A MICHIGAN MEMOIR

Jim McGavran

Michigan State University Press
East Lansing

♾ The paper used in this publication meets the minimum requirements of ANSI/NISO Z39.48-1992 (R 1997) (Permanence of Paper).

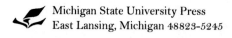 Michigan State University Press
East Lansing, Michigan 48823-5245

Printed and bound in the United States of America.

16 15 14 13 12 11 10   1 2 3 4 5 6 7 8 9 10

LIBRARY OF CONGRESS CATALOGING-IN-PUBLICATION DATA
McGavran, Jim.
  In the shadow of the bear : a Michigan memoir / Jim McGavran.
    p. cm.
  Includes bibliographical references and index.
  ISBN 978-0-87013-981-9 (pbk. : alk. paper) 1. McGavran, Jim. 2.
Journalists—Michigan—Biography. I. Title.

  PN4874.M48397A3 2010
  070.92—dc22 [B]   2010003514

Cover design by David Drummond, Salamander Hill Design

Book design by Scribe, Inc. (www.scribenet.com)

ℊ green press INITIATIVE Michigan State University Press is a member of the Green Press Initiative and is committed to developing and encouraging ecologically responsible publishing practices. For more information about the Green Press Initiative and the use of recycled paper in book publishing, please visit www.greenpressinitiative.org.

Visit Michigan State University Press on the World Wide Web at:
www.msupress.msu.edu

To my parents,
Jim and Mamie

James Holt McGavran   Marion Jaeger McGavran

1910–1994   1910–2001

CONTENTS

PART ONE

THE WAY BACK

Five miles north of Empire, after the turnoff from M-22 to M-109, I slowed and began looking for the two-track to The Ritz. I knew where it ought to be, but there was no break in the emerald wall of trees. Confused, disappointed, I rounded a curve out of the forest into an open meadow. I looked right, down a long grassy field that sloped towards Little Glen Lake, and then, through a row of small pines, I saw it.

I had pictured a roofless, windowless ruin, lost to fire or neglect— or worse, bright and fresh and irredeemably tawdry, a Holiday Inn Express risen like a huge tin-and-glass mushroom in its place. But The Ritz was there. With more eagerness than prudence I pulled off M-109 and parked on the shoulder. My wife Deje waited in the car while I strode down the hill into a scene that my brain immediately video-recorded in slow motion. As I got closer, I saw that the old cottage was not only still standing, but much improved: the siding was aluminum now, the drafty front sleeping porch had been glassed in, and propane tanks by the chimney meant there was heat.

Suddenly the back door opened. I couldn't move; in fact I could hardly breathe—paralyzed, caught between fear and the surge of a wild, impossible hope. A blond woman in white shorts and halter-top stepped out with strange, rapid grace like a dancer,

1

a bird, a spirit. She looked around in all directions, but seemed not to see me. Then, as quickly as she had appeared, she vanished around the corner of the house.

For a moment I felt pure terror. I remembered my father telling me of a dream in which his older brother came to him and said he would take him to their mother, who was in the next room. Dad knew even as he dreamed it that it was a death-dream. Both his mother and his brother had been dead for decades—my pretty, vivacious grandmother that I never knew taken by a heart attack just about the time of my conception, and my uncle in 1961, well before his time. Dad believed that he would have died had he let his brother "take him to Mother," so he did the sensible thing and woke up. I wasn't dreaming the cottage that afternoon. And I had never believed in ghosts, though I know my parents did. But for that moment I actually thought the door of The Ritz would open again and my parents would come out to greet me, their smiling young faces tanned golden from days spent on the beaches, and ask their now-aging firstborn child in for a manhattan before dinner. Make that two manhattans; Mom always said you can't fly with one wing.

Earlier that same sultry afternoon in July 2001, we had followed M-72 west from Traverse City across the southern edge of the Leelanau Peninsula and on into Empire, while roads opened in my brain that I had kept closed over half a lifetime. At first I couldn't react; I could only observe the old white clapboard houses huddled close to the sidewalks, the big trees shielding them from the heat as they would from winter storms, the dooryards exuberant with daylilies, delphiniums, and hostas. As I drove on down Front Street, Deering's Market and the Friendly Tavern appeared on the left—just where they belonged, I caught myself thinking—still sharing the same low cinder-block building, but with a seventies-style façade of bricks and shingles that was new to me but easily a quarter century old. By now I was hearing voices in my head—scratchy and faint at first, like a faraway AM radio broadcast playing in the dusty dashboard of a '52 Ford. Was that my mother I heard arguing with Deering's butcher about the price, or the freshness, of the hamburger? Whose was that beery laughter that seemed to rise from inside the tavern, punctuated by the tap-slide-and-clunk rhythms of a fifty-year-old shuffleboard game? Had my father just delivered one of his witty asides?

My hands started to shake on the steering wheel, and I said something—I have no idea what—to Deje as I guided the rental car to the end of the street, turned first to the right and then to the left, and found the beach road just where it was in my brain, where like Deering's and the Friendly it had been waiting for me. In tears now, I drove down the narrow old road towards the water; but I laughed out loud when I saw the huge, ragged cube of concrete still squatting in the middle of the parking lot. Defying gravity and scraping our knees, my brother Fred, my sister Molly, and I used to climb all over this apparently unmovable remnant of the pre-World War I glory days of the Empire Lumber Company.

Next came the wide beach itself, and beyond it, the lake we had swum in so often—the "big lake," we always called it; we only said "Lake Michigan" when we were talking to friends at home who had never seen it. Deje and I got out of the car and walked onto the sand. The magnificent views had not changed: look left, and you see the Empire Bluffs rising steeply out of the lake; look right, past Southbar and Northbar lakes, and the great Sleeping Bear Sand Dunes, equally steep, glow peach gold through the summer haze. But the picnic tables were not where I remembered them. Worse, I couldn't locate the small dune overlooking the water where my father stood when he played his accordion for us on those long-ago August evenings. But I recognized the rainbow colors of the small stones glistening by the shore—black, gray, blue, ochre, pink, red, even green—like the ones we stubbed our toes on when we ran on the beach as kids. Stooping to grasp a red one, I saw it was heart-shaped and, like many of the others, etched with strange lines—a cursive I still wish I could read, quirkier than Cyrillic, as exotic as Arabic. I handed it to Deje because in the past we used to share these geological love tokens with each other.

Lost between time zones, emotionally jetlagged, I needed Deje's help to know what to do next. We decided to drive north out of Empire to the Sleeping Bear climbing face, so I could show her the view of Little Glen from the top. But we didn't make it to the dunes parking lot that day; the reopened road in my brain stopped just a few hundred yards short when I found The Ritz—and my parents' ghosts. Because I did find them, I was sure of it: they were in there; I had cornered them. Caught off-guard by the spirit's warning, they knew it would kill me to see them, so they stayed put, that's all. They wanted to come out to me, I could feel it—I can still feel it.

Somehow I managed to realize I couldn't hang around the cottage any longer. I had started back up the hill, through the tall grass towards the car, where Deje was waiting, when a butterfly flew up to my eye level, hovered there a moment, and then fluttered away. From its bright orange and black wings I immediately knew it to be a Monarch, both ephemeral and hardy, a migrant across borders and waters. It flickers in my brain still—an image not only of my parents' spirits, but of my own, and of those of all of us brave enough—or foolish—to seek to reopen our lost cerebral pathways, to soar free of our everyday entrapment in commerce and custom, to find the places that connect us to our lives, our selves.

The Monarchs don't make it back to Michigan from their winter home in Yucatán; it's their descendants, perhaps their great-grandchildren, that "return" to Leelanau with the warm weather. Still I envy them: when they're ready to migrate, they just flap those outrageous sun-dazzle wings and go. For my family, getting ready to leave for Glen Lake in the old days replicated on the domestic level the original triumph of divine order moving over the face of the deep as chronicled in Genesis 1. My mother, the primary force against chaos in this case, kept a list of what we took to The Ritz each year so that she and Dad could collect everything—the thermoses, the sweaters, the blankets stowed in the attic—and he could start packing the car the night before we left. There were additions and deletions every year, and Dad's creative packing skills—and no doubt his patience—were strained simply to find room for everything Mom said we needed. How could I know then that a generation later, history would repeat itself when Deje and I packed our station wagon to head to North Carolina's Outer Banks with our kids each summer?

Statuesque and strong at 5' 10", my mother strode purposefully through my early world, easily role-shifting, almost shape-shifting, from involved PTA parent, to aproned supercook, to diligent evening seamstress, to perspiring summer gardener, to white-gloved church lady, to bejeweled life of the party. The daughter of one of Mom's best friends remembers her even in old age as "stately," "a lady who always looked regal," but with "a good sense of humor" too. Centered and secure in her marriage, wrapped in the love we all shared, she lived her life fully, grandly, and joyously nearly all the time. "Nearly" because sometimes demons beset her—in the form of worries and fears whose source I have never determined. Like Mrs. Bennet in *Pride and Prejudice*, she would sometimes complain that her "nerves" were bothering her. These "nerves," which my father did not joke about, though he was at least as clever as Mr. Bennet, could bring sudden volleys of criticism directed at whatever or whoever caught her attention—excepting Dad, that is. Without warning she might burst out angrily at her eggbeater, her vacuum cleaner, the venetian blinds—which she hated because they were hard to dust—or us. If we were inside reading or playing cards, she would say she was tired of seeing us laze about—we were too weak; we wouldn't grow up right—and make us go outside "to get some fresh air and exercise"; but later she might come out and order us back into the house because we were "making too much noise" or "going wild." If we protested, she would reply with expressions that we came to know well, and that meant all such complaints were futile: "None of that truck!" she would say loudly, or the briefer but sharper "No back talk!"—or, even more succinctly, "Pipe down!" Later, in our teen and college years, she would not scruple to enlist the Bard's help, melodramatically quoting Lear's lament that an ungrateful child is "sharper than a serpent's tooth."

As I said, Dad was never the target of Mom's sudden angers. Undemonstrative, often shy in strange company, but with a heart full of love for her and for us, Dad witnessed her outbursts, but never criticized her about them; he knew, I think now, that she didn't really mean them and regretted them when they occurred. But maybe he should have said something. Perhaps Mom needed him to respond more strongly to her car packing or other demands—even to complain. Perhaps my father, who wrote Mom brilliant love letters the summer before they were married, retreated too much into himself at times. In all the early years with them, the whole time I was growing up, I never once heard them fight. In fact, I must have already been sixteen or seventeen when I heard a friend's parents get into a spat one evening while I was over at his house. Hearing their raised voices terrified me; I honestly thought they were about to get divorced, and I began to feel sorry for my friend and wonder if they would have to move. Now that nearly all their generation are gone, I can only wonder how Mom and Dad managed the apparent serenity. I know, because Mom often reminded us, that the minister who married them had counseled them, in the far simpler manner of seventy-plus years ago, never to go to sleep angry or with anything important left unsaid between them.

"Nerves" or not, Mom expressed strong, even unreasonable opinions on many subjects. "Dope fiend" was one of her kinder names for Judy Garland, the talented but troubled star who played Dorothy Gale in the Hollywood version of *The Wizard of Oz*. Mom "wanted no truck" with some of Garland's methods of flying beyond the rainbow; but regardless of the Judy Judgment, she loved the Oz stories. As a girl growing up on the East Side of Columbus, Ohio, in the teens and twenties of the last century, she had avidly read the entire series of L. Frank Baum's Oz books. A generation later, Fred, Molly, and I reread the old, broken-spined copies she had carefully saved for us. And we knew the movie almost by heart: "Toto, I've a feeling we're not in Kansas anymore." "Pay no attention to that man behind the curtain." "I'm melting, melting—what a world!" "Why Dor'thy, you've killed her!" "Oh, Auntie Em, there's no place like home!" So every August at vacation time, while Dad backed the heavily laden car down the driveway very slowly, so the bumper would not hit the street, Mom channeled Judy long enough to lead us in a rousing chorus of "We're Off to See the Wizard." We loved this ritual of departure and sang as loud as we could from the back seat, but we always got confused about the "If-ever-a-Wiz-there-was" section and just repeated the "We're off" part in an increasingly cacophonous canon until Mom had had enough and told us to pipe down. Of course our destination was not the Emerald City, but a tight little coldwater cottage hidden deep in Leelanau's green forests. And once we got to The Ritz, she never got mad at us the way she sometimes did at home. She was different there.

I will need all the help I can get—the Scarecrow's brain, the Tin Woodman's heart, the Cowardly Lion's courage, and a bit of wizardry as well—to continue this story of my parents, our long-ago vacations, our everyday lives in Columbus that framed the annual getaways, and my long-delayed return to Leelanau after my parents' deaths. Like Dorothy Gale—like all of us—I need to feel I belong somewhere in the world. With a click of her red-shod heels, Dorothy found that place back home in Kansas with Auntie Em and Uncle Henry. I found it within myself by losing and then reconnecting with Leelanau, a place that has shaped both my past and present life far more than I could ever have realized had I not returned there when I did.

It was a simpler world my siblings and I grew up in. Things we accepted and even enjoyed in 1949, when we first went to Little Glen, seem today almost as primitive as Thoreau's cabin at Walden Pond. The Ritz had indoor plumbing, but there was no hot water except what Mom boiled on top of the electric stove in the tiny kitchen. Apart from the stove, the big fireplace in the living room gave the only heat. There most assuredly was no television. And Mexican migrant workers, not mechanical shaker-harvesters, picked cherries in the Leelanau orchards while we vacationed. One day when we were in Empire grocery shopping, we saw three small men with black hair and skin the color of Dad's new Lucky Strikes before he smoked them. They were standing at the side of the road, looking at a dusty old truck that had a flat tire. Fred, Molly, and I had never seen people like that before, golden tobacco-leaf people, and we must have been staring at them. When one of the men looked right into my face with hard black eyes, I was suddenly afraid. Then Mom was pulling us towards our car and whispering: "Those men are Mexicans. They come here each year to pick the cherries. Don't look at them." She herded us into the car and Dad drove off. My white middle-class parents shared many of the ethnic and religious prejudices of those days, and it's possible that Mom's actions were based on contempt for the Mexicans. But she may have felt a sympathy with their flat tire and their poverty that she couldn't express; like many of her generation, she had studied French but not Spanish. Besides, she was always telling us how impolite it is to stare at anyone.

At home in Columbus, things were different too—not as primitive as The Ritz, but quaint. No Mexicans were around, but the milkman came twice a week. It cost three cents to buy a purple Jefferson stamp to mail a letter. Mr. Finch, our mailman, with his kindly old eyes, brought us bills, Christmas cards, and letters from my aunts and grandparents, but never an L. L. Bean catalog or a request to renew our Sierra Club membership and receive a tiny polar bear toy as a thank-you gift. There was not a stereo, but a monophonic radio-phonograph in the living room, where we played 78 rpm recordings of Broadway shows, hillbilly—oops, country-and-western—music, and opera arias. And if one of us got sick, Dr. Matthews not only made house calls, he came right up to our bedroom to look down our throats and make us say "Aaah!"

But supposing I get the *Back to the Future* details right—the cars, the clothes, the Lucky Strikes, the music—there's the distance issue, a distance of years and of hundreds of miles. To tell our early story, I must tell my later story of rediscovering Leelanau, and to do that properly I must confess that for over four decades I stayed away. The physical distance between Leelanau and my adult life in North Carolina has certainly played a part. But it's more than that. On a bright Carolina summer day, one relatively free of Southern humidity, I might remark, "Why, this is Michigan weather!"—but I wouldn't stop to recall how I knew what "Michigan weather" was. Having returned annually since 2001, I now know that I repressed my Michigan memories, and that I repressed them because I feared their power. And while it was wrong to straight-arm them, some of them, as you have seen, are extremely intense.

Please don't misunderstand that last sentence. I continue to wonder about the tensions that may have flowed below the calm surface of our family life, but as much as I might speculate about Mom's mood changes and Dad's emotional distance, I have no juicy family scandals to report. As a child I was often rebuked, and if I did something really bad I was spanked, but I was never either abused or neglected; like Fred and Molly, I was loved. If either or both of my parents were addicted to alcohol, drugs, gambling, or extramarital sex, it was done in secrecy and I was too innocent to have any idea of it. Fred and Molly were similarly naive, or I assume I would have learned from them of any parental peccadilloes they are aware of. But part of our childhood innocence is its inability, or at least its extreme disinclination, to admit worldly experience if it doesn't affect us directly. Children, moreover, usually have a vested interest in believing the best of their parents and may even refuse to hear a parental confession when one seems imminent. I actually managed to do that once when I was well into my fifties.

There's yet another issue—residency. I may as well blurt it out: to this day, past and present, I have been only a summer visitor to Leelanau. That fact alone, for some, will deny me the right to say anything about the beautiful, isolated peninsula west of Grand Traverse Bay. How dare I sing the sun-gilded beauties of July and August when I have never weathered a November storm off Lake Michigan, never slogged to school or driven to work in

Empire or Glen Arbor through dirty late-March snow—no skis, no skates, no one-horse open sleigh?

Apart from the obvious retort that winter is at least as much a state of one's mind and relationships as it is of meteorological phenomena, I must point out that we had some memorable cold-weather events in Columbus back in those days. The famous Thanksgiving blizzard of 1950 comes to mind, when Michigan beat Ohio State in the "Snow Bowl," as it is still called, at the OSU stadium just five miles from our house in Upper Arlington, while we built an igloo in the front yard. Besides, Leelanau's history, its reputation, and its economy all have depended for over a century on the memories of tens of thousands of summer migrants like my family and me. And not just us tourists. Remember the Mexicans who came to pick the cherries. Remember the Odawas and Ojibwas who trekked in and out seasonally for millennia before settling at the reservation in Peshawbestown, on the Grand Traverse side of the county. Remember the Monarchs and all the birds that still fly north every summer. We came too—neither to work nor to stay permanently, but to enjoy the two weeks of my father's vacation in a place like nowhere else on earth. It has always been a long day's drive to Leelanau, and like Oz, it most often has seemed not a reality but a dream, a bright dream of summer seen through the dull grays of our long Ohio winters.

It looked like a black-and-white movie outside. The snow was white, the trees were black, and everything else was gray. I could hear the gas furnace roaring in the basement, but the cold seeped in through the leaky steel window frames my mother hated almost as much as she hated the venetian blinds. As I looked out, heavy frost on the panes suddenly blazed with the headlights of a passing car. I was afraid of the cold.

From the kitchen table, my father called me to show me an envelope. Mr. Finch had brought it that day through the snow. Except for the purple stamp, the front was entirely covered with large, wobbly writing. The round postmark said "Empire, Mich." The man who wrote it, Dad told me, was Mr. Salisbury. He owned The Ritz. Dad told me the letter was a receipt. It meant that Mr. Salisbury had received Dad's deposit check. He would reserve The Ritz for us in August. Dad wanted me to know that we would return to Little Glen.

I was confused at first. Summer and Glen Lake seemed so far away on that bitter winter night. And my economic sense was so undeveloped that I had never thought about having to pay to stay in the cottage. I wondered how the letter had come so far in the terrible weather. I felt the weight of a father's duties that I would take up for my own family someday. But I was no longer afraid of the cold and the frozen windows. I felt happy and safe, because I had a smart father who arranged things.

In sixth grade we did reports on foreign countries. Mrs. Workman let me do Australia. I loved Australia. I wanted to go there. It was far away, halfway around the world from Ohio, but the people spoke English, so if I went there I would understand them. Except for "Qantas," the Australian airline. In English you weren't supposed to have a "q" without a "u" after it. I wondered if other "q" words in Australia didn't have "u's." Would an Australian write "qick" instead of "quick"? "qote" instead of "quote"? When I saw ads for Qantas in my parents' *New Yorker* magazine, I always wanted to write in the "u." In fact I did it once, but they failed to notice—or if they did, they were not moved to comment.

Australia was in the Southern Hemisphere. This meant that since it was winter in Ohio, it was summer in Australia. All the books called it the "island continent." It was ringed with beaches, and the beaches in the pictures looked beautiful. The only beaches I had ever seen were on Glen Lake and Lake Michigan. So while I wrote my Australia report, I started thinking about my secret beach.

I found it one summer because Mom said I was old enough to take the rowboat out alone. Little Glen was so shallow near the shore, she said, that even if I managed to hurl myself out of the boat, it wouldn't be over my head. Besides, I could swim. I had already passed three Red Cross swimming tests—pollywog, turtle, and waterdog—at the old swimming pool next to Upper Arlington High School, and Mom had sewn the badges onto my bathing trunks.

I lifted the heavy anchor, lowered it into the boat, and pushed off from the low dock. I swung the oars too deep at first and stirred up clouds of sand on each side of the boat when they hit the lake bottom. Then I didn't swing the oars deep enough and they splashed water across the surface of the lake. I was what was politely called a "poorly coordinated" child—a klutz, in other words. But finally I must have swung them just right, because the little boat began to move.

It was a hot, bright August afternoon on Little Glen. Sunlight sparkled on the tiny ripple-waves that looked like fish scales spread over the top of the lake. It sparkled another way in the swirls the oars made in the water. I was glad to be alone, away from the others. I rowed straight out from the shore, looking to the left every few seconds. I knew where I wanted to go: down the lake towards the highway. But first I had to row out far enough to clear another dock that was longer than ours. When I got far enough out, I turned the boat to the left. I rowed past the long dock and followed the shore.

I was journeying to claim my special beach. I knew it was there. Riding home from Deering's that morning, I had seen it when my father turned the car from the highway into the sandy two-track in the trees that led to the cottage. It was a smooth, secret strip of sand, invisible unless you looked at just the right moment.

Before long, I found it. I rowed the boat right into the shore until I felt it scrape in the sand. Then I threw the anchor down and jumped out onto the beach. On the right side, trees grew out over the water. You couldn't walk there without bumping your head. Tall, thick grass grew out of the water on the other side, so you couldn't walk there either. But right in the middle, there was a space about as wide as our center-hall house in Columbus—as wide as a living room, a front hall, and a dining room.

I walked from one end of my beach to the other a couple of times. There were no footprints but my own, and none of the many-colored stones we found at the big lake. The water was so clear that if you looked at it from a certain angle, so it didn't catch the light, you couldn't tell where it stopped. I sat down on the sand. It was my own beach, my own Australia. The thought excited me, but mostly I felt peaceful. Then I thought about buried treasure and how I didn't have a shovel. But I didn't want there to be treasure, not really: I wanted to be the first person ever to come there. I thought about standing a big stick up in the sand to mark it, to claim it as my own. But what if someone else saw my stick and decided to come and claim the beach for himself? I didn't want the other boys I played with at the cottage to find it. They would want to play war there, the way they did on top of the sand dunes, with plastic toy guns and old army water canteens. I stayed at the beach for a few minutes longer. It was quiet except when a car passed behind the trees on M-109.

Then I thought I should go back, so Mom wouldn't worry. I put the anchor back into the boat, pushed the boat off the sand, and got in. My weight made the boat stick in the sand again, so I had to get out and push it out farther. I rowed back up the lake towards our dock. Rowing away was bad and good. It was bad because I was leaving, but it was good because I could watch it while I rowed. I continued to watch it inside my head as I finished my Australia report.

That was me—the timid, sensitive boy who feared the January cold, the dreamer who found himself a private beach, the scholar who wondered about "q's" without "u's," the Columbusite whose favorite place in the world was a remote Michigan coastline that he saw once a year as a child and then forgot about for decades. From 1949 until my high-school graduation ten years later, we always spent the first two weeks of August at Little Glen. Then education, marriage, and career pressures intervened. After a B.A. at the College of Wooster, a year in France teaching conversational English, a master's degree at Columbia, and two years teaching at William and Mary—where I met Deje, another English instructor—I began doctoral studies in British literature at UNC-Chapel Hill, got married in 1968, and finished my Ph.D. in 1973. That led to my teaching job at UNC Charlotte, Deje is now a professor at Queens University of Charlotte, and we have spent nearly all our adult lives in North Carolina, well beyond easy driving distance to northwestern Lower Michigan. Instead, Deje and I took our own kids—Catherine, Mark, and Jamie—on vacation to the Outer Banks, another beautiful, fragile region of sand and wind and water. I returned with Deje to Leelanau five months after my mother's death, motivated partly by a vague desire to pay her and my father homage there, but mostly by the fact that Cathy, a physical therapist, had taken a job in Ann Arbor, thus giving us both a reason to head north and a convenient stopover. Since then, not only Cathy but Mark, a software engineer for Bank of America who has also emigrated to Ann Arbor, and Jamie, a Ph.D. in Russian literature now teaching at Kenyon College, have also traveled to Leelanau with us.

The Ritz sat on Little Glen almost literally under the shadow of the Sleeping Bear. There were five of us in the old days—five people, that is. Our dog Mickey, who was part boxer and part not, joyfully accompanied us to Leelanau and managed to spend much of his time there soaking wet—and soaking us when he shook himself off. The huge brown mohair sofa in the cottage also seemed imbued with animal life. Loose springs assaulted our lower bodies whenever we sat on it; odd creaks and sighs were heard; and ancient odors, awakened from the sleep of time, wafted up as we warmed ourselves by the fire.

It was, as I've said, a long trip from Columbus. We left at six in the morning and drove all day with the windows open in those un-air-conditioned, pre-interstate days, through the Ohio cornfields and the sleepy little towns full of churches and gas stations. When we crossed into Michigan just west of Toledo, Mom had a song for this threshold moment, just as earlier she had sung Judy's *Wizard* song. This time it was "We Don't Give a Damn for the Whole State of Michigan, We're from O-Hi-O"—a brash ditty sung to the tune of "The Old Gray Mare" that for generations has delighted xenophobic Buckeyes and visited apoplexy upon enraged Michiganders. I remember how I loved getting to sing "damn" out loud since this was a "bad word" we were usually forbidden to use. After this, it was more heat, more wind, more cornfields, more sleepy towns. For some reason, we often got lost in or around Clare; and as if to prove that the poltergeists are still active in the area, Deje and I managed to do it again just last year. But once past Cadillac, as we approached Leelanau, the cool, dark northern forest gradually surrounded us, enticing and mysterious as in a fairy tale.

Mom and Dad tried in vain to find an arrangement of three kids and a dog, in the back seat of the Ford Ranch Wagon my father borrowed from his boss, that would do away with territorial disputes and other, subtler forms of sibling rivalry. Seatbelts were still a decade and a half away, so we tended to stretch, slip-slide, or simply poke our way into someone else's space. I could almost always stir up trouble by driving one of my miniature TootsieToy cars over the seatback into Fred's or Molly's hair, or onto the book one of them might be reading (I got carsick and threw up when I tried to read in the back seat, so I wasn't allowed to, but I didn't like for them to get away with it). Depending on the decibel level of my siblings' response—it had to be loud enough to be heard over the rush of air from the open windows—a warning growl or "Pipe down!" might be forthcoming from the front seat. Another effective gambit we all used was to begin whining that it was our turn to sit next to Mickey and put an arm around him. All three of us loved the dog, and it was fun to sit next to him and share his so-many-smells, so-little-time joy in the ride. But as we knew only too well, his saliva blew back onto the face of whoever sat next to him, so that actually sitting there was far less enjoyable than the thrill of hearing from an exasperated maternal voice that it was one's turn to do so.

We usually managed to reach Little Glen in time for a cooling-off swim before supper, after stopping first at Deering's to add several bags of groceries to the already crowded back seat. Hitting the lake for the first time each year, after the long, hot drive, produced a delight almost fearful in its intensity—simultaneously a banishing of the cares of home and a baptism into the joy of the coming days. I still remember my little sister's thick blond braids glistening in the late-afternoon sun, and my brother's pale shoulders that would be sunburned by the next day, and how we sometimes felt, or thought we felt, or argued about whether we felt, fish in the water bumping against our bare legs.

Later, after Mom fed us—maybe hot dogs, maybe creamed chipped beef on toast, and fresh Leelanau cherries for dessert if

Deering's had them in—we sat for a while on the old sofa by the fire to get warm. Then we got ready for bed, and Dad tucked us in for the night on the sleeping porch of The Ritz, just as he always did at home in Columbus. In the strange, cold Michigan darkness, life seemed stripped to its essentials, and those essentials seemed clear and clean and good. As I lay bundled up and waiting to fall asleep, I listened to the wind and looked out at thousands of stars we never saw in Columbus. Where had they all come from? Canada, maybe? On the road map in the car, Mom had shown me that Michigan was close to the Dominion of Canada, a foreign country, and it thrilled me to think that Canadians might look up and see the same stars. As I grew sleepier, I would mentally map the bright blue-sky, blue-water days that lay ahead: climbing the sand dunes, swimming in Little Glen, picnicking at Empire Beach, or—if it rained—shopping for postcards and souvenirs in Glen Arbor at the Totem Gift Shop, which for some reason none of us remember, we nicknamed the "Hollywood."

At the time I was jealous of classmates who took summer trips to places like New York, Washington, or the Grand Canyon and bragged about it in Show-and-Tell the first week of school. I too longed to see the latest Broadway musicals; it was the heyday of Rodgers and Hammerstein, and I loved their witty, tuneful, but socially conscious shows like *South Pacific* and *The King and I* and played the original-cast recordings over and over again on our phonograph. I too wanted to visit the Lincoln Memorial, where "Fourscore and seven years ago" was carved into the marble walls, and where the great black contralto Marian Anderson sang after the Daughters of the American Revolution refused to let her sing in their hall. I too yearned to see the great Colorado River rushing through the bottom of the canyon—and I still haven't seen it, except from the air. The first time I flew to the West Coast, back in the seventies, the pilot announced that we could see the Grand Canyon off the left side of the aircraft, and the plane practically tipped over as many of those on board followed my brainless lead and leapt leftward to see the huge rust-colored gash in the earth.

But no; for us it was always Glen Lake. Everything stayed the same, year after year—the lake, the cottage, the stars, the dunes, the deer we saw grazing in the meadow at twilight. Even the postcards in the Hollywood didn't change. I couldn't talk to my father about this at all—it would be like accusing him of not making enough money. And if ever I dared to bring up the subject with Mom, I was silenced by a "No back talk" look and the irrefutable argument that we "just couldn't afford trips like that" with their expensive hotel bills, ticket prices, and restaurant meals. It took forty years of absence for me to realize what a precious gift my parents gave us with their limited means—the gift of time in a beautiful place that would live in us forever if we nourished it.

Time is but the stream I go a-fishing in. I drink at it; but while I drink I see the sandy bottom and detect how shallow it is. Its thin current slides away, but eternity remains. I would drink deeper; fish in the sky, whose bottom is pebbly with stars.

With words as his fishing line, Thoreau seems effortlessly to connect earth and heaven, time and eternity. Following his transcendental hint, I continue my memories with a fishing trip—a bit perversely, since I don't like to fish and haven't done so more than once or twice since this excursion at Little Glen well over half a century ago. The last time I tried it, I paid too many tourist dollars to take our son Mark trolling in Albemarle Sound, just inside the Outer Banks. I got seasick and spewed Coca-Cola all over the deck of the boat, to my own disgust and that of the crew, while with grace and tact Mark ignored his wretched father and hauled in several excellent bluefish, which Deje pan-fried for dinner that night.

With apologies to Michigan fishing writers from Jerry Dennis to Jim McVey, this Leelanau fishing trip was not about father-son male bonding. It was not Dad, but my mother who got us up early one morning to go fishing before breakfast. Daybreak was the moment, she told us, when the perch and bass in Little Glen would be most likely to bite. So we bundled up in jeans and jackets against the dawn chill, trooped down to the dock, and clambered into the rowboat. Mom, Fred, and I took turns rowing—Mom first. My father, who didn't enjoy fishing any more than I did, stayed at The Ritz with Molly.

When it was my turn, Mom said to try to row very gently and quietly to avoid scaring the fish. Clumsy as I was, I rowed noisily, even managing to bang an oar against the side of the boat. I was repelled by both the abstract concept and the physical reality of attaching a worm to a fishhook; Fred was highly attracted to this same idea and activity. We must have scared the fish, because we didn't catch many; Fred got one or two, but Mom pronounced that they were too small to be "keepers" and threw them back into Little Glen. At the time it seemed a botched excursion. I was disappointed, embarrassed about my physical awkwardness, and sleepy from having gotten up so early.

But all that fades out of mind now, and I remember the early-morning quiet on the lake, the tall marsh grass under the shadow of the trees along the shore, the mist rising as the morning brightened, the great dunes becoming visible above the tree line to the left, and to the right, the Alligator, the forested hill of reptilian profile that separates Little Glen Lake from Big Glen, where richer people owned or rented bigger summer houses. And I remember my mother's beauty and authority as she led this expedition—determined, I see now, to set it like a jewel in the platinum haze of the morning and hand it to us to keep. If she could only know how well she taught us. It wasn't just about fishing; it wasn't even mostly about fishing—but is fishing ever really mostly about fishing? It was about self-control and learning how to do things right—things God knows I still need lessons in; and it was about honoring the beauty of the world—the life we are given and the places we live it in.

And so I continue to try, at this remove of time, to form some "grown-up," informed idea of my mother, and of how the two weeks at Glen Lake changed her from the high-energy, dutiful, but moody fifties wife and mother—the target of Betty Friedan's later feminist denunciations—into the cheerfully commanding woman who taught us the rigors and pleasures of fishing, boating, beach picnicking, and dune climbing. I wonder if she herself was conscious of the transformation. I never thought to ask her, but I do know that she had no use whatever for Betty Friedan. In fact, by any estimate, Betty vied with Judy Garland for a place near the top of Mom's rather extensive life count of cultural undesirables. If I employ the politically correct language of the present time, I may wonder whether Leelanau freed my mother from the confining gender-based routines of home. Maybe; but perhaps its waters and beaches simply put her in touch with bright memories of her younger self—of long summer days spent at her family's cottage on Buckeye Lake, east of Columbus, or of her honeymoon with Dad at Fire Island, New York, after their wedding in September 1936.

But if I am right about Mom's transformation, then I must wonder what my father thought of it—and whether our trips to

Leelanau changed him as well. Speculation becomes more difficult here because, like many other men of his generation, Dad, who was shy to start with, tended to hide his feelings or express them indirectly by employing the ironic sense of humor that always made our McGavran family reunions so much fun. Did he, like me, feel cowed as well as charmed by living in the shadow of our transformed Michigan Mamma? I think that for him, admiration won easily. I don't know what he did that morning when Mom took us fishing, but I like to imagine he slept in and dreamed of her—the woman to whom he wrote those passionate love letters, his life partner, the mother of his children. We still have a striking photo of her descending the Sleeping Bear, wearing jeans and a red-and-white-striped pullover with a big sailor collar that we called her Gina Lollobrigida shirt in homage to the sexy Italian movie star of that era. Mom is smiling right into the camera, her eyes are sparkling with excitement and the heat of the exercise, and no one but my father could have taken that shot.

However reserved he may have been with his emotions, Dad was an artist—with both words and music. If our Leelanau Augusts calmed Mom's "nerves," empowering her to throw off the social restraints of Central Ohio ladyhood and assert herself more freely, they must also have nourished my father's growth and confidence as the writer who published essays in the *Saturday Evening Post* and later became a local celebrity for the humorous "Professional Old Man" column he wrote weekly for the *Columbus Dispatch* from his retirement until shortly before his death in March 1994.

Dad was also a fine amateur pianist. As a teenager, he had accompanied the silent movies that came to Cadiz, his small Eastern Ohio hometown; and although he read music well, he could also play by ear. No World War I or World War II farewell songs, and few old standards from Broadway or Tin Pan Alley, were unknown to him. A cool performer under his veneer of diffidence, he sometimes entertained or played sing-along at the parties he attended with Mom at home in Columbus. About the time we started going to Little Glen, he bought his squeezebox, a little old German accordion that I still have and play, in a pawnshop in Columbus, and he always brought it with us, so that even without a piano he could still play anything that the simple little Hohner's six chord buttons would allow.

He and Mom were beautiful people—tall, dark-haired, magnetic, charming in company—like characters in the Scott Fitzgerald stories they read at OSU in their college days. In movie-star terms, Mom was a stronger, bigger-boned version of Rosalind Russell; and with his dark brown eyes and vaselined black hair Dad looked more than a little like Clark Gable, who was actually another Cadiz boy like himself. Though they never had much money, Mom and Dad went on glamorous, risky journeys in the early years of their marriage. To visit Mom's sister in Boston, they once drove all the way from Columbus in an old Studebaker named Arthur that got vapor lock in the Pennsylvania mountains and had to be backed up the hills—or towed. Then they saved up and spent the weird, scary year before World War II erupted going around the world on a British freighter. It was a long, exciting second honeymoon, but Dad wanted to try his hand at fiction writing, and they thought the isolation on board would help his concentration. They made friends with their cabinmates—other adventurous young couples like themselves. They debarked at ports of call such as Durban and Shanghai to buy what today we would call multicultural *objets*—an elegant mahogany African head; a graceful, smiling Chinese Guanyin with a movable hand—that we used to touch gently and marvel at as kids. They weren't back in the States for long before their freighter

HMS *Chinese Prince* was sunk by a Nazi torpedo early in the war. I can still see Mom crying over the kitchen sink when she told us that the captain, who had befriended them with his gracious British manners, was lost along with his entire crew. It must have seemed to both my parents like the burning of Eden, a final expulsion from carefree youth and joy. Still, they kept something of their Fitzgeraldian glamour about them well into middle age.

So perhaps it is not forcing memory too strongly for me to see my parents as king and queen of a particularly Northern, particularly Midwestern Carnival—not a New Orleans-style Fat Tuesday in February, but Fat August in Leelanau—as they shed their ordinary roles as editor and housewife to lead the revels for us and the friends from home who stayed with us on Little Glen, sometimes sharing the Ritz with us, and gathered at our evening picnics at Empire Beach. Inspired at these events by a couple of manhattans or beers, Mom would become still more extroverted, the life of the party. Sometimes she danced in the firelight, laughing with the other grownups, after we had grilled and eaten our dangerously high-animal-fat hot dogs or hamburgers. The only time I saw her dance at home was the evening she put on a peach satin flapper dress, complete with three rows of fringe below the dropped waist, which she had worn as a teenager to her oldest sister's wedding in Columbus in 1926. I remember how excited she was that after thirty years and three children she could still get into that dress. The fringes shimmered against the satin; she had a twenties-style headband in her still-dark hair; she was gorgeous; and she did the Charleston for us in our living room before going out to a party with Dad. I asked her to show me how to do it, and she did, but I couldn't get the hang of it, either that night or for years afterward.

While the other grownups at Empire Beach sang along in harmony, Mom's thin, clear soprano rose somewhat incongruously from her tall, robust frame, and Dad accompanied them, playing the sun down on his accordion. As the light sank and the wind on the beach got colder, we all waited to see whether a big old ore freighter would steam along the horizon just in time to be silhouetted against the setting sun. Whenever one did, we all cheered wildly—as if miles away across the water, the crewmen would hear us and yell back.

Since the Hohner had no minor chords among its six, the songs Dad played sounded cheerful. And some of them were indeed happy, even funny, like "When the Red, Red Robin Comes Bob, Bob, Bobbin' Along," which I later played four-handed with him on the piano at home. But many of the lyrics were not. They spoke of departures, great distances, uncertain returns—of love's yearning in the face of war's mortal dangers: "It's a long way to Tipperary, and the sweetest girl I know"; "There's a long, long trail a-winding into the land of my dreams"; "Now is the hour for me to say goodbye"; "We'll meet again, don't know where, don't know when."

Of course, it can be argued, these sentimental songs are only part of a nation's war effort, a form of pop-culture propaganda created to romanticize the self-sacrifice and pain of the many and feed the coffers or the egos of the few. Their simple melodies and harmonies make them easy to learn: they're pretty. That these things may be true does not detract from their ability to express some of the deepest feelings we all have—feelings that as a child I hadn't yet known. Such feelings transcend intergenerational issues, gender issues, war and peace issues to speak to our knowledge of our temporary status on earth and our almost inexpressible longing for contact with those we love who are absent: "Smile the while I bid you sad adieu, / When the clouds roll by I'll come to you." As kids on the beach at Empire, we began to learn of the glory and pain of life before we were quite awake to them—physically, emotionally, or intellectually—in our own lives. And in spite of all the accordion jokes you've ever heard, there is something grand, romantic, and heroically life-affirming in a man who stands on the beach at twilight, flinging his music into the wind and the oncoming dark—so his wife and their friends could sing the songs they loved, and so his kids would learn them and the lessons they taught. If I ever develop Alzheimer's, I will forget my own name before I forget the words of the songs my father played.

In Leelanau, Deje and I found out, there is good news for the visitor. Much of the former beauty of the place still exists: one does not have to arrive as I did with a head full of memories to delight in the loveliness of sun, sand, water, orchard, field, and forest. Thanks to a largely fortuitous combination of local zoning controls and low population for nine months of the year, big-box stores and fast-food restaurants even now have barely begun to appear—although Traverse City has sustained a major hit. If you look down on Little Glen from atop the Sleeping Bear, you see no high-rise time-shares breaking the emerald tree line around its shores. Farms and orchards are being sold off; development has occurred and is occurring—at the Homestead resort in Glen Arbor, in Empire, in Suttons Bay, and elsewhere around the peninsula, just as it has for the century and a quarter that Leelanau has been a tourist destination—and some of it is pretty hideous. But at the same time, much seems unchanged, even pristine. This illusion of stability and timelessness is largely the result of the federal takeover of the sand dunes and adjacent lands near the big lake—ironically, a most unstable environment both geographically and economically. The creation in 1970 of Sleeping Bear National Lakeshore has proved a great boon for summer residents, tourists, and environmentalists, but at the cost of a long, painful, and divisive process that has left some local landowners still embittered.

Everything is relative, however. If we think historically about land grabs in Leelanau, we must note that on the reservation at Peshawbestown live descendants of the men and women who were there before there was such a thing as real estate in North America. What their continuing bitterness may be, even in the face of their recent casino profits, I do not presume to tell. To them also, though they surely wouldn't put it this way, "belonged" the animals the first French trappers came to kill and sell for furs, and the forests the Anglo and Norwegian and Bohemian settlers came later to cut and sell for lumber. It seems to me, naively perhaps, that tourism, if properly managed, will not become so rapacious as those earlier industries, if only for the simple reason that if Leelanau gets over-developed, not more but fewer people will want to visit or reside there. All we ever wanted, and all that most other tourists then and now want, is to come and enjoy it, leave it as good as we found it, and then come back—again and again—so that once we bond with the place, we will not forget how it has taught us about who we are. Through its attempts to balance public and private concerns, the National Park Service has managed to recreate some aspects of the Native equilibrium of natural and human life that existed before the rest of us arrived.

If Native Americans "own" Leelanau at all, it is through the stories they have told about it. The most famous of these is the legend that has named the dunes. Here it is, as retold by Empire-based writer and teacher Anne-Marie Oomen:

The great She-Bear, Mishimokwa, . . . left the shores of Wisconsin with her two cubs and swam across Lake Michigan. When she pulled herself onto the shore here in

Michigan, she turned back to call the cubs, but they slipped in exhaustion under the waves and drowned. She was so filled with grief she tore open a place in the land, then in her own exhaustion, fell asleep watching for them to return. The Great Spirit sent a golden wind which covered her with sand. She sleeps still, watching and waiting for her cubs. Because their journey had been so valiant, the Great Spirit raised the cubs and changed them into two beautiful islands and named them after himself, North and South Manitou.

The story is as simple, and as primal, as that: a mother's challenge to her children, and her heart-stopping grief when they failed and she lost them. The name "Sleeping Bear" did not originally apply to the entire dunes area, but just to one forested knoll atop the rest that resembled a bear in silhouette when viewed from the big lake. This knoll has so seriously eroded in the last century that it no longer seems bear-like. But ironically, instead of dying out, the name now includes the entire stretch of the dunes, from just north of Empire all the way to Glen Haven—and beyond that, the entire lakeshore.

Whatever joy or pain we know in life, the stories we tell about the people and places we love can flow like water, like the wind, like the blood that courses through us with every beat of our hearts—reviving us, sometimes even changing us as the Sleeping Bear legend changes our understanding of the dunes, as Leelanau changed my mother and father, and as I feel myself changed by catching a few bright memory-fish such as these I am sharing. Armed with stories, with the wizardry of language, I proceed both forward and backward, struggling to become a cartographer of the past as I steady my gaze into those Leelanau waters—so brilliant, and often so deep.

PART TWO

SHADOWING MOM

The morning after we found The Ritz, it was "Michigan weather" for sure in Leelanau. Here on the forty-fifth parallel, halfway between the equator and the pole, bright sunlight painted Van-Gogh-in-Provence color everywhere we looked. The field grasses and wildflowers danced in a lively breeze; gone was the humidity that only the day before had seemed capable of harboring ghosts. Today was for the present, for Deje and me, not the past.

After breakfast, we decided to go for a hike, so we took M-109 north past the dune climb and down into Glen Haven. The sight of the big lake as we crested the hill, just past the old Day farm, took my breath away as it did years ago, when I saw it over my parents' shoulders from the back seat of the Ranch Wagon. We coasted down the steep hill into Glen Haven, turned left in front of the old red and white canning factory, passed the Coast Guard station and maritime museum, and parked at the Sleeping Bear Point trailhead.

We trudged a couple of hundred yards, taking a right fork uphill towards the lake while our legs and feet labored to maintain forward momentum in the soft sand. Then we stopped still, over-come—with recognition on my part, Deje with the awe of the first-time visitor. We had just stepped into one of Leelanau's most spectacular wraparound water views, at close to 270 degrees. Here at the north edge of the dunes, wide headlands frame the big lake's more-than-Mediterranean range of indigoes, sapphires, azures, and aquas, while on the horizon, green and alluring—like two Bali Hai's, two lost Atlantises—float the North and South Manitou Islands, the drowned cubs of Mishimokwa the Sleeping Bear.

Vistas like this one usually delight me, but today I began to feel sad—old, defeated, unimportant. As we continued on the trail, a young couple with a baby in a backpack caught up with us. We chatted for a moment; then they asked us to photograph them with their camera. We did, they reciprocated with our camera, and later, when we saw that shot (we still used a film camera then), we experienced the generation gap in a big way. Although we pride ourselves on being reasonably well-preserved, Deje and I look almost decrepit in that photo, with the brilliant sand and the big lake behind us—not least because seeing those happy young people with their baby reminded us that Jamie, the "baby" of our family, was at the time already almost twenty-two.

So this day too began to call me back to the past. And I realized that from the moment we stepped awkwardly onto the sand, I had been hearing my mother's voice playing contrapuntally in my brain against what Deje and I were saying to each other. This was not the returning spirit I had both feared and desired the day before, but the remembered sound of Mom's voice—firm, almost cross, yet heavy with her care for us: "Don't run up! You'll be exhausted. The harder you take each step, the more you'll sink backwards into the sand. Go slowly but steadily and you'll reach the top sooner."

This maternal voice is my primal memory of our Leelanau vacations. Forever linking my mother in my mind with Sleeping Bear, it both precedes and follows the fishing trip on Little Glen and my discovery of my private beach. Like a sergeant with new recruits, like a mother bear with rambunctious cubs, my mother in her sternest mode is giving us our marching orders. I don't know where she learned it. She could not have had much previous experience with sand dunes—certainly not on the flat sidewalks of East Columbus, where she grew up. Of course she was right, and whenever we did as she commanded, we got to the top of the climbing face sooner, were less winded by the effort, and had more time to enjoy the splendid view back across M-109 to Little Glen.

Not only here and now, I began to understand, but whenever and wherever I have climbed sand dunes, I have heard her voice— teaching me, coaching me, preparing me. She has been there every one of the countless times I have climbed the Jockey's Ridge dunes with our children at the Outer Banks of North Carolina. I even heard her in France in 1964, at the Bassin d'Arcachon on the Bay of Biscay, where I climbed the great Pyla dune during the year I spent teaching English conversation in a lycée in Bordeaux. As long as I live, wherever I go—by the pyramids of Egypt or in the deserts of Australia—whenever I see sand hills, I know I'll hear her.

Even without a mother's voice to chide and encourage, many other Leelanau vacationers would choose a visit to the dunes on such a morning. As much as orchards, beaches, or forests may attract, Sleeping Bear forms the most striking geographical feature of the peninsula. The highest moving sand dunes in the eastern United States, they rise over four hundred feet at a slope of 34 degrees—as steep as sand can rise—from the eastern shore of Lake Michigan. Geologists call them perched dunes to distinguish them from beach dunes, which consist entirely of sand. These dunes are literally perched atop a terminal moraine left by a retreating glacier during the last Ice Age. The moraine, a huge pile of debris—boulders, gravel, sand, and clay—rose thousands of years ago, creating Big and Little Glen Lakes by dividing them from the big lake. At the bright western edge of Leelanau, the dunes are like a desert, like the moon, like heaven, like nothing else in the Midwest. Hiked in summer and skied in winter, they can be seen from the Empire Bluffs and the beach, from Little Glen, from Glen Haven, and of course from the islands and boats on the big lake. Jack Lousma, a Michigan-born astronaut, even spotted them from outer space. The Pierce Stocking Scenic Drive affords less physically active visitors priceless views of the area; and the dune climb off of M-109 draws carloads of visitors each year now, just as it did when I was a boy.

The downside of all this human activity on the dunes is not difficult to imagine: deforestation, erosion, and speeded-up migration of the dunes themselves, all of which require the vigilance of National Lakeshore personnel and other scientists to maintain even a semblance of stability. This is why the dunes look so much greener than I remembered them: the government has planted acres and acres of grasses, flowers, and other ground covers to slow the drifting of the sand. As early as 1950, ecologist Frank C. Gates was deploring the tourist activity on the dunes—first on foot and on horseback, then, starting in 1940, in "dunesmobile" cars equipped with special fat tires—that had already caused irreparable damage to the once-bear-shaped pinnacle dune that gave the entire area its name. Little did any of us think, the one time my frugal parents splurged and paid for a dunesmobile ride, that we were contributing to the degradation of the awesome but surprisingly fragile Bear.

It is their geological uniqueness, their vulnerability, and their strange beauty, along with their enormous economic importance as a focus for tourism, that drove the determination first of Michigan officials, led by Governor William Milliken, and then of the federal government to declare the area a National Lakeshore. This designation, granted in October 1970 by an act of Congress, has saved thousands of acres from runaway development and thus preserved an invaluable heritage for the future. But the land-acquisition process necessarily differed in Michigan from parts of the West, where many of the great national parks were carved out of previously unsettled lands. In Leelanau, where farms, orchards, and vacation homes have long abounded, "more than 1400 tracts of privately-owned land had to be acquired to create the lakeshore"; moreover, according to Theodore Karamanski, "a heavy-handed, poorly planned land acquisition program reinforced the bitterness that surfaced during the decade of struggle that preceded authorization." Thus, in order for millions to be able to enjoy the dunes, hundreds of landowners were dispossessed of lands so deeply connected to their individual and family lives that they experienced not only a financial loss, but an emotional amputation.

One lakeside cottage owner, David Hacker, lamented the loss of "a strip of beach and a handful of acres that once gave a family identity"; the Hackers had lost their sense of belonging in the world that I have found in my own life by reconnecting with Leelanau. Glen Arbor native Kathleen Stocking has eloquently expressed many residents' feelings:

> It is incomprehensible to people born and raised in Glen Arbor that throngs of summer visitors—people in Winnebagos, people from Ohio or Florida or Maine, who come for a day or a week—will ever understand the daily rhythms and moods of the place where they grew up, a land that is part of them and they of it, a land for which their feelings are so close to the bone that it is almost impossible, if not improper, for them to be articulated.

How does one begin to tell someone that they don't want to move from the dunes because the stars there are closer to the earth than anywhere else in the world? Or that the quality of light on a clear day in mid-August brings the Manitou so close to the mainland that it seems one could reach out and touch them?

While I cannot heal the pain of Hacker, Stocking, or other long-time residents, I can say that we returned to Leelanau each summer precisely because of those dunes, those stars, those islands floating offshore like nothing else in the world. That was how my parents created the memories I am now attempting to recover. The constant tourist traffic into and out of the area seriously threatens some permanent residents' sense of self and place. Yet it brings many of them their livelihood, and it brings back people like me who are more than willing to pay the going rates to revisit the land of their memories and dreams. Since the demise of the logging trade nearly a century ago, and the fur trade long before that, tourism in its various aspects—fishing, boating, swimming, hunting, hiking, camping, golfing, skiing, shopping, dining—has remained the most important industry of the peninsula. Although no one there has ever made us feel unwelcome, I know that emotions still run deep, and that whether—and how—the conflict between locals and outsiders can be healed is still being worked out in Leelanau.

As Deje and I continued on the trail from Sleeping Bear Point that day, we saw the Manitous over and over again. I have seen many maps of Leelanau, I have taken the daily boat trip to South Manitou several times—both islands now are parts of the Lakeshore—and in the rational side of my brain I do not forget they are only a few miles away. But as the Native legend affirms, these islands have always worked powerfully on the human imagination. And this morning, across the brilliant waters of the big lake, they didn't seem close at all, but as insubstantial as a mirage in the desert. In spite of what I knew to be true, I believed that they would recede further and further if I tried to approach them. What they represented, what they were trying to say to me, as I stared across the water, seemed complex and contradictory; and it lay both outside and within me. In a reversal of the Ojibwa myth, my dead parents were now the islands and I the child yearning, from the shore, to reconnect with them. But I also saw in the islands an image of myself as I now felt, psychically split in two, divided between past and present, death and life. Either way, if it wasn't a total loss, it was something that had cracked apart and needed to be glued back together.

We walked on and found ourselves descending into a basin where we lost both the breeze and our view of the islands. We saw sand and very little living vegetation, for we had entered a "ghost forest," where the ever-moving dunes had exposed the petrified spines of huge, ancient conifers they smothered ages ago. The stripped-bare, sharp-pointed silvery gray trunks retained only vague notches like vertebrae where branches once fanned out. No longer growing straight to the sky, many leaned at bizarre angles— emblems of chaos and collapse, and perhaps, my imagination whispered, of danger as well. It suddenly occurred to me that a giant strong enough to extricate these huge trunks could hurl them like spears to pierce our hearts and leave our bloody corpses for carrion feeders down in this airless hollow.

Climbing the far side of the basin and once more catching the breeze, I found that my death-fantasy blew away as quickly as it had arrived. As we circled further inland on the dunes, we could look back across and see the islands again—and once, when we looked over our right shoulders, we briefly glimpsed Little Glen shining bright as a turquoise in the clear air. We had begun once more to feel the heat from the warm July sun when we descended a steep hill into a hardwood forest right on the dune, its cool shadows fragrant with an abundant vegetable life they could hardly contain—ferns, wildflowers, brambles. Just as we saw parked cars through the trees and knew the hike was nearly over, a satiny orange day lily by the path caught the sunlight, and we stooped to marvel at it. What was it doing there? Just what we were, I guess—living joyfully on the trail. With beauty, mystery, and strange hints of menace, Sleeping Bear had put her best foot forward to greet Deje and to welcome me back after my long exile. And although bereft of her since her death earlier that year, I had heard my mother's voice.

As a returning visitor to Leelanau, I can't claim the intensity of feeling of local residents who have lived their entire lives in the dunes' shadow. Still, for all of us, the ecological and financial importance of the Lakeshore is both driven and immeasurably enhanced by the imaginative value we find in them—by the stories they tell us, and by those we tell about them. We narrate our geography, especially anomalies like the dunes, because finally we can't help it: we need to give to extraordinary, otherwise overwhelming places a human shape that we can wrap our thoughts around. But even as we do so, the dunes in reciprocal fashion shape our thinking, leaving an imprint that far outlasts our tracks across their fragile, wind-etched surfaces.

Back in the 1920s, a local writer, Harry R. Dumbrille, both reiterated and intensified the personification implicit in the ancient Native story. His best-known poem begins with a much-quoted line: "Oh, Sleeping Bear, what dreams must come to you!" Dreams of parental love, dreams of parental ambition: the story of the mother bear and her two cubs unites the

affective and exhortatory sides of child-rearing while reminding us of the inevitable losses that even the warmest, most
supportive family relationships can neither prevent nor even
forestall. Another of Dumbrille's poems, "Sleeping Bear
Pinnacle," again evokes the dead mother's love and grief for her
lost children—and theirs for her as well. He imagines all three
of them caught somewhere between dreaming and waking,
death and life: "Will not the great storms as they beat round
your lair, / The lightning's forked flash, as it goes through the
air, / The shock of the thunder, arouse you from sleep? / The
call of your loved ones out there in the deep?" It is this in-
between existence, both thrilling and depressing, that overtakes
me when I look at the islands.

Anne-Marie Oomen has taken the story to another level,
mindful that the name "Sleeping Bear" originally applied just to
the small hill atop the main dune—the lone, forested pinnacle
that from the big lake looked like a recumbent bear and thus
drove the Ojibwa legend. When she visited the spot on a cold
winter day several years ago, Oomen saw that the pinnacle, once
robust with the life of the trees that grew on it and gave it its
ursine shape, had become a concavity, a sepulchral bowl like a
smaller version of the ghost forest Deje and I traversed: "And
from that basin her bones rise—bleached, long-dead tree trunks
scattered and leaning and stunning. The remnants of a forest are
cast about like ribs and femurs and spine in the silence." The
erosion of the pinnacle, although rightly deplored by environmentalists, does not diminish but actually enriches the Native
legend, for it adds the disturbing image of a womb not only of
life, but of death. I think of the Hindu goddess Kali—the great
and terrible mother, alternatively nourishing and baleful—
because of my mother's power over my own siblings and me.

In this context, my own addition to the developing story may seem small, as futile as a drowning bear cub's squeal for help, as fleeting as a footprint in the sand on a windy day. It is simply that just as I hear my mother each time I climb the dunes, whenever I recall the legend of the Sleeping Bear, I hear her telling it. As a child I found this sad, reassuring, and at the same time vaguely frightening. She told us the story every summer in our younger years—always formally, seriously. At least once, I remember, I heard a catch in her voice—a sign that she too felt its power deeply. By reminding us of the fierce love and ambition of the grieving mother bear, she could speak indirectly of the complexity of her own love for Fred and Molly and me, and how it must always be intermixed with challenge, with discipline, with expectations, and with chance—in short, with teaching. As a young child, unable to express any of this, I remember that I used to wonder instead what it would be like to become an island. It mostly seemed terrible. I wouldn't be able to move; I would have to float motionless in the water, growing colder and colder until I froze to death like Leonardo DiCaprio in *Titanic* (granted, that comparison was not available to me when I was a child in the fifties). But maybe, somehow, I could get used to it, the way we did when we swam in the big lake. Would I still hear and see? I would need a face for that, and islands don't, as a rule, have faces. And so it went.

With Deje, I looked out once more at the Manitous. Dividing them from us and from each other were wide stretches of water—inviting, radiant in the sunlight, but fatally cold and deep. The islands, and the self-knowledge they promised, remained psychically inaccessible to me. The mythic locations kept reversing, but the gulf remained, or even widened. Mom, my larger-than-life mother, fierce and protective as a bear, strong-looming like a mountain of sand—and Dad with his wit and his shyness, and the past, and the self-knowledge I so longed to recapture: it all lay far out across the water, across space and time. I wondered whether, when I die, I would figuratively cross the water and become part of the mystery that those who survive would contemplate as I do now. But I also knew I was looking at the emblem of a past I would continue to pursue and explore.

Two years later, Deje and I were on our third return visit to Leelanau—two and a half years after my mother's death, and more than nine years since Dad died. A year after a big reunion in 2002, when Fred and Molly came with all their families, my brother and sister-in-law drove up again from Cincinnati to visit us at the house we rent in Cedar. On a close July morning, while Deje and Liz chatted at the house, Fred and I decided to hike the short trail to Pyramid Point. Rain was forecast, and we could feel it in the air. But the high clouds glowed mother-of-pearl bright as we took the Port Oneida turnoff from M-22, drove past the old school and farmhouses, passed through the grounds of Camp Leelanau, and parked at the trailhead. Brothers in our sixties now, lawyer and professor, we were eager to spend as much time together as we could, and the coming rain did not concern us. Besides, we both felt the bond of the land itself—the forests, fields, sands, and orchards of Leelanau that connect us to our childhood and our parents.

We walked through the tall grass on the trail that would lead us into the forest and, in about a mile, to the Pyramid Point overlook, one of the most spectacular in the Lakeshore. The milkweeds' thick, bulbous clusters of purple bloom were starting to fade, but knapweed carpeted the meadow in lavender, and small clusters of outrageously bright taxicab yellow flowers appeared here and there as we walked along. We said little for a while: we both knew that Mom loved wildflowers, so we didn't have to speak about it—fortunately, since we both seem to have inherited her quick emotional responses and might well weep if we tried. I began recalling silently how Mom would exclaim about them whenever we went for a drive in the country outside of Columbus, and how often as children we all made day-long picnic trips to state parks, sometimes with our McGavran cousins from the other side of Columbus. It seems to me now that on these trips, as on our annual treks to Leelanau, Mom left her demons behind.

It felt like spring in Columbus, but it was cold in the Ohio woods. I put my hands inside my jacket pockets, but it felt funny walking that way, so I took them out again. Besides, there weren't leaves on most of the trees yet, so sometimes the sunlight came through and warmed the path. I was walking near my mother. All of a sudden she shouted, "There they are, mayapples!" She lunged ahead of me and pointed to the left. I looked and saw some shiny, low plants. They looked like umbrellas for chipmunks. Mom bent over them and reached her fingers gently under the leaves. When she lifted them, I saw the small white flower underneath, grow-ing in the fork between the leaf-stalks. By this time, Fred, Molly, and Dad had caught up with us. "Look, look!" she repeated delightedly. "You really have to look to see the flowers. They seem shy, don't they, hiding under the big leaves."

We all walked on. Mom was euphoric. She showed us wild violets, bright purple stars blooming on the ground around us. Of course we had seen them ourselves, but we enjoyed her excite-ment and took another look. She was looking for a trillium, a wildflower with three petals as its name implies, but she couldn't find one; she said they were rare and only bloomed briefly. Then she lunged again with another happy shout. "Look, Jimmy," she said to me, "you'll like this one the best; there's a story about it.

See—it looks like a minister in church giving a sermon." I looked where she pointed. Was it really a flower, or just a twisted leaf? It was the strangest flower I had ever seen. It had a vertical tube with a flap at the top of it. She gently lifted the flap, and I saw the little thing inside. "This is a jack-in-the-pulpit." Mom was right. Now it was my favorite flower.

Fred and I continued towards Pyramid Point. Then suddenly, involuntarily, I stopped in my tracks. In a small tree in the meadow, I saw a flash of blue so intense that I was stunned; then I felt summoned, called to attention. I touched Fred's arm and pointed where to look. It was as if from somewhere between the aquas near the shore and the deep purples farther out, a small piece of the big lake had taken solid form and flown over the dune to us. It had to be a bird, but a bird beside which the brightest blue jay would show as a delicate pastel. Unfazed by our approach, it stayed in the tree long enough for both of us to have a good look at it. Then it jumped to another perch in the same tree, lingering again before it flew away.

At the house later that day, we found a copy of Peterson's *Field Guide to the Birds* and quickly identified the bird as an indigo bunting. The illustration left no room for doubt; but the shock I felt was only partly dispelled by the calm descriptive language of the ornithologist. For as Fred read aloud from the guidebook, I recalled Mom, in some long-ago moment, praising the buntings' beauty. She too must have seen them during our Leelanau vacations, but perhaps they also showed up at home in Columbus, where she put feeders out every winter for years. An environmentalist before it became fashionable, she loved birds as well as wildflowers. She kept a life count of the birds she had seen—and she always chased cats from around our house. I couldn't help wondering once more about ghosts. Had she sent us a sign? Or was that our mother herself appearing before Fred and me in the bunting's form? I couldn't tell, but the path seemed the one we should be on.

Mom's love for us, deep down, was wild, animal-like, even ursine: she was mother-bloom, mother-bird, mother-bear. As her buds, her chicks, her cubs, we knew we could absolutely rely on her for support and protection. She embraced her parental duty passionately; she would defend us and never abandon us. In Michigan, she always kept a sharp eye on us when we swam, whether in Little Glen or at the big lake. At home, if someone teased one of us at school and we told her, she was furious; if it seemed serious, she would call the teacher. When I cut my finger open on a broken glass in the kitchen and my blood dripped dramatically onto the counter, she appeared immediately with the bright orange disinfectant and the Band-Aid box, promising me that my injuries, however threatening, would not prove mortal.

Every December in Columbus she took us downtown to see the electric trains and Santa's workshops in the big Lazarus department store windows. Part Auntie Mame, part orphanage matron with a military background, she hovered over us to herd us along and fend off the holiday crowds on the sidewalks. She had us all hold hands whenever we crossed the street, and she would speak sharply, sometimes pulling us forcibly back into line, if one of us loitered or showed any tendency to wander off. She practically dared danger to appear—and thus scared it off most effectively.

This ferocious side also appeared whenever she watched an Ohio State football game. She regarded it as an intolerable affront if an opposing team ever gained yardage against the Buckeyes, let alone scored. At these moments, in spite of her internalization of "polite lady" behavior, she could often be heard yelling, "Get him!

Get him! Kill him!" at the television screen. Mom had played basketball in high school and certainly did not lack competitive
spirit. If she ever secretly wished that Fred or I had lettered in
football or basketball for Upper Arlington High School and OSU,
she kept those disappointments to herself. And besides, it was
Molly who turned out to be the athlete of our family: she became
a fine tennis player and still wins doubles tournaments in Alberta
with her husband John.

Mom always came to school if there was a performance or an
award involved. Delighted, she and Dad led the applause when we
all went to a junior-high talent show to hear Fred play a solo version of "Unchained Melody" on his bass horn from the marching
band. They came to all my choir concerts and to our high school
production of Rodgers and Hammerstein's *Carousel*, where I played
the Starkeeper and had to pretend I was wise as God while perched
on top of a rickety ladder that scared me to death. One morning my
senior year, I saw my parents and Molly sitting in the gym as I
marched in for a student assembly. I was amazed to see Dad away
from his office in the middle of the day, and right away I realized
what it meant: I was going to get one of the awards to be handed
out that day. I told Mom later that I was glad they had come, but
that it took away the surprise of the award to see them.

When they called her from the school to tell her I was going
to receive another award at another assembly, she and Dad decided
not to go. I'm sure they wanted to see more glory heaped upon me,
but they didn't want to spoil my surprise. As insensitive as I was
then to Mom's powerful emotions, I finally understood this—but
not soon enough. When I came home that day and told her about
the award, I could tell that she already knew about it, but I was
stupid enough to wonder out loud why she had not bothered to
attend the assembly. She started to cry. I could perform acts of

contrition to my last breath, do community service at Habitat for Humanity until they sent me away for knocking holes in the sheetrock—I never could drive a nail in straight—but I still can't forgive myself for saying that to my mother.

The other side of her fierce love was that sometimes, like a mother bear cuffing her cubs, she lashed out at us in anger or frustration. Were these her "nerves," her inner demons, or were *we* her demons? Fred and I certainly earned many of these rebukes; we often acted more like fleas getting into her skin than cute, fuzzy bear cubs, while Molly, bonding closely with Mom early on, instinctively distanced herself from the bear-baiting activities. Fred took the lead in directly challenging her authority; it was he who didn't get dressed on time for school, ran outside and got dirty before church, or made idiot faces when she was taking family snapshots. My preferred role, the cause of a subtler rupture of the domestic tranquility, was that of the good, obedient child who waged secret passive-aggressive warfare. Even as a very young tyke, I could—and did—raise her blood pressure by telling baby Fred not to eat something she had fixed for us: "Don't eat it, Fweddy," I would say in my kiddie lisp; "it's concusting!"

I have no idea why I said such things; there was never any reason to attack Mom's cooking. She was an excellent cook, she loved to cook, and she worked hard at it all year long. Even in Leelanau, where she kicked back and relied heavily on fifties staples like hot dogs, bologna, and processed peanut butter, we always had fresh fruit and vegetables to be sure we got all our vitamins. In June, when the strawberries got ripe in Ohio, she would make a layer-cake-sized shortcake biscuit, split it, and stuff it and strew it with fresh berries and whipped cream. That night we would have strawberry shortcake for dinner—an entire dinner of dessert. I quickly grew to love this concept; in fact I still love it. In July, as soon as corn on the cob was available, she drove at least twice a week to the edge of Upper Arlington to a vegetable stand that sold just-picked corn on the cob. Well into old age, she would denounce any corn that was over a few hours old; it was part of her Ohio pride. After our return from Glen Lake, she spent long August evenings in the steaming un-air-conditioned kitchen, with Dad's help, canning tomatoes, peaches, and green beans for us to eat the following winter, and slapping away the sparrow-sized State Fair flies that proliferated in Columbus during the dog days.

For Christmas she baked rich, buttery shortbread cookies, which she rolled thin and cut out in the shapes of Santas, reindeer, pine trees, and wreaths for us to sprinkle with colored sugars and the bright cinnamon Red Hots that we used for eyes and holly berries. There were cornflake-raisin cookies, which also got sprinkled; rich German cookies made of ground almonds, sugar, and egg whites, but no flour; and the "ball" cookies—white snowballs rolled in confectioners' sugar, and brown bourbon balls coated with chocolate sprinkles. Then there were date-nut pinwheels. I always teased her about these because I didn't like the overripe flavor of the mashed dates that got rolled up, with the nuts, into a long spiraling cylinder of dough that she sliced to make the individual cookies. Of course it didn't stop me from eating them.

In January, no matter how vile the weather, she would drive all over town in search of a fresh coconut—not the easiest item to find in Columbus in midwinter in those days—so she could make Dad's favorite cake for his Age of Aquarius birthday. He always helped her, first hammering a nail into the coconut so she could drain out the milk for the cake, and then cracking the whole thing for the "meat," which she put into the major-artery-clogging frosting. Those cakes were amazing.

As we continued on the Pyramid Point path, I stopped my silent reminiscences long enough to tease Fred about the "nice egg" he had eaten for breakfast before we started out. I think that I had bacon and a scrambled egg that morning too—though I usually resist these high-fat temptations. In any case, the expression "nice egg" has a long history in our family.

Year after year during our school days, Mom asked us every morning at breakfast whether we wanted a "nice egg." I know why she did it—I knew it even then. She loved us and wanted the world to know it. Unlike certain slatternly mothers she could (and often did) mention by name, she rose with her children each day to get them off to school with a good breakfast inside them. And once up and dressed, she wanted to be more than the silent witness of our juice-gulping and milk spills: she wanted to be actively engaged in promoting our welfare. Fred, kinder to her on this issue than I, went for the egg more often. But I never thought there was anything very "nice" about a yolk leering up at me from the plate, so I almost always held out for a bowl of Kix or Cheerios or Raisin Bran. Besides, I loved to mail in quarters taped to cereal box tops and then stalk the mailbox for weeks until the promised toy appeared. But as time passed, I began to hear both pain and a hint of menace behind Mom's repeated offer, so I would say yes to an egg once in a while—and chew lots of toast while the egg bites were in my mouth, to minimize their eggyness.

My antifeminist, anti-egg paranoia was latent in those halcyon days; it has since blossomed, as Deje knows only too well, into a theory that women deliberately tempt the men in their lives with eggs in order to jack up their cholesterol and eventually kill them. Looking back now, I can see how inevitable it was that Fred and I both began to tease Mom about her use of the expression "nice egg." Naturally she resented this baiting, and naturally Fred and I were too dumb to do anything but escalate it once we saw how effective it was. "Pipe down!" and "No back talk!" began to be heard more frequently at breakfast time. I don't remember which of us first realized the potential of a mockery of eggs that would also ignite her suspicions regarding the Church of Rome—we were Presbyterians—but sooner or later it had to happen. One of us (Fred says it was me) called her, to her face, "Our Lady of the Nice Egg." This provoked a terrible fury, which I will not attempt to describe except to note Mom's enraged insistence that she was not, nor would she ever suffer herself to become "Our Lady" of anything. Some time later, after I had spent my year in France, I could make Fred giggle nervously, if we were at home together, by whispering under my breath "Nôtre Dame de l'Oeuf Gentil"; but I never dared to say this out loud to Mom. Besides, it sounded even dumber in French.

Psychologists tell us that children of divorcing parents often blame themselves for the breakup and suffer from feelings of guilt and low self-esteem. My parents' marriage never seemed to me to be in trouble, but I generally assumed that if either of my parents got angry with me for any reason, it must be my fault. As you have seen, many of the little games Fred and I played with Mom were indeed blameworthy—though I don't think we fully realized how annoying we were. But as I grew older, I began to realize that Mom's sudden anger could also come without external provocation or warning. These were the times when she would say, as an apology, that her "nerves" bothered her.

I still recall a moment in our kitchen when I was probably a junior or senior in high school. I was standing in front of the stove. I don't remember what I was doing; I may have been boiling water for tea or waiting for some toast to pop. Mom walked in and yelled at me for no reason I could fathom. I suppose it could have been something one of us had done or left undone earlier that day, or it might reflect some deeper source of anger long forgotten or repressed. She could have seen my standing by the stove as a threat to her power as food provider—or simply as an invasion of her space. Although I am not generally known for presence of mind in a showdown, I actually called her on it. Not accusingly but calmly, I said something like "Why are you angry? There's nothing wrong." To my utter confusion, she began to cry and said, "I don't know."

Pop psychologists today would be quick to attribute this to PMS or menopause, but I wonder whether there was a deeper issue. Today my mother, who like many of her generation loudly rejected psychiatry, might be diagnosed with depression or bipolar illness and put on medication. But whether or not Mom suffered from an emotional disturbance of some kind, I will take a cue from her arch-nemesis Betty Friedan and speculate that if the problem lay to some degree in Mom's brain chemistry, it may also have been the result of her partly chosen, partly dictated role as post–World War II housewife and mother.

Still, even as I write that, I have qualms. When the book appeared in 1963, Mom found Friedan's attack on the feminine mystique blatantly, hatefully offensive to someone like herself who was living it with so much energy and gusto every day. After all, she was a brilliant, creative woman who had written poetry in college, assisted an interior designer in the depths of the Depression until she had to be let go, made and decorated ceramic ware in some evening classes she took while we were growing up, worked hard in her flower garden every spring and summer, belonged for years to a Great Books club that met regularly to discuss classic texts, sewed many of her own clothes and Molly's, made me a red and blue clown costume for Halloween when I was eight, and learned to make ratatouille the hard way from Julia Child's

Mastering the Art of French Cooking (although she knew French pronunciation, she always called it "rataTWEEL"). And she did meticulous crewel and needlepoint work well into her eighties; one old friend remembers that Mom was already aging when she made a needlepoint kneeling cushion for weddings at Boulevard Presbyterian Church. When our children were born, she would hop the first plane she could get from Columbus to Charlotte so she could help us out at home while Deje recovered from labor and delivery and established a breastfeeding schedule. As strong-willed as Mom was, what Deje remembers is how consistently she deferred to Deje's opinions, and how deftly and cheerfully she cooked, cleaned up, and generally made things easier for us all.

No, she never simply wallowed in the stultifying domesticity reviled by Friedan, nor did she engage in what today we would call Martha Stewart–type feeding frenzies at local stores to acquire darling "must-have" stuff for her house; she couldn't afford it, but she would have disdained it in any case. In the allegedly fetid backwaters of fifties domesticity, she always had several projects going. Reasonably enough, she would occasionally ask one of us to help her out around the house or yard—something we were not always either willing or even able to do. Oh, sure, I could always handle picking up my toys or my side of the bedroom Fred and I shared. And when we were older we all were happy enough to jump into the car and run errands for her at the drugstore or supermarket: any excuse to "have to go out in the car" was most welcome.

But I also remember her asking me at least once to weed her large garden, which ran the length of the driveway from the street all the way back to the garage behind the house. As a man, guided by her example more than I could ever have imagined, I have become an enthusiastic gardener—and so have Fred and Molly: we all now love to dig holes, get dirt under our fingernails, plant things, and tend them. But back then, I couldn't understand why she cared about it—though I loved the botanic pun when Mom told us of a girl she had met at summer camp years ago who insisted on calling forsythia "forsyphilis." I remember her passion for irises, and how each autumn she would order a few new rhizomes from a nursery in Oregon, and how anxiously she waited through the winter, and how disappointed she would be if one of them failed to bloom properly. And I remember being out on my hands and knees on a hot, humid summer day more typical of North Carolina than Ohio, trying to find and pull weeds, and just hating it. Whether in ignorance or in malice I can't say, but I actually pulled up some "good" flowers as well as the ubiquitous dandelions and crabgrass. Eventually she must have given up on me, because I don't recall having to do it often.

She was not a gambler, but one time she entered a contest and it paid off big-time. We got to come home early from school one day to hear Garry Moore, emcee of a popular national television program, announce that "Mrs. James McGavran of Columbus, Ohio," had won a hat designed by then-famous French milliner Lily Daché. She had been notified that her name would be announced on the air that day, and she wanted us all to hear it and share in her triumph. Dad watched on a TV at his office. Following the rules of the contest, whereby a different hat winner was chosen every week, Mom had submitted a snapshot and description of herself and the following original rhyming couplet: "I'd be as chic as a clipped French poodle / If Lily Daché would equip my noodle." I remember that outrageously sassy rhyme, and I remember the day the hat arrived in a huge pink box sent all the way from New York City. It was a wide-brimmed navy straw hat with tiny pink roses set on one side of the low crown, and Mom was thrilled:

not only did it suit her tall, angular good looks, but she already had a navy suit to wear it with. Still, I think the poem mattered even more to her; it was through her verbal wit that she had won the hat. It was the equivalent of Dad having one of his essays or stories accepted for publication.

Her great energy notwithstanding, I think it is a little too easy to look back now and say that Mom needed a job outside the home, a career, and that she would then have been happier, more "fulfilled." She seemed totally invested in the gender role her times imposed on her. She worried about becoming a mother for over four years after marrying Dad, submitting to numerous painful tests before becoming pregnant with me. Then, once she had given birth to us, she was unable to nurse us. Of course doctors and nurses were not as supportive of breastfeeding as they are now, but I know, because she told us, that it was a terrible disappointment to her. As we grew up, she regularly attended PTA meetings, and she was active with Fred and me in the Cub Scouts, and with Molly in the Brownies and Girl Scouts. She made it as easy as she could for Dad to pursue his writing vocation in the evenings, when he would work on articles and short stories.

But she may indeed have felt frustration under the surface, and I wonder now whether Mom was secretly or even unconsciously jealous of those few of her friends who held jobs. If so, she expressed it indirectly by saying almost condescendingly, if ever the subject came up, "Isn't it too bad that Mary Jane (or Virginia) has to work?" There were at least two major ironies here. The first was that even then I could see that Mary Jane and Virginia had a kind of self-confidence about them that my mother, for all of her aggressive strength, lacked, and that could very well have come from their sense of their own success not only in making money, but in balancing the professional and domestic claims on their time. The second irony was that we could certainly have used the money. Dad's work as writer-editor of a small magazine never paid him what he deserved for the magazine's continued success, or much more than what we middle-class Middlewesterners needed. We ate well because of Mom's cooking, canning, and careful planning, and we had a comfortable though smallish house; but there were few frills, except for those Glen Lake vacations—and as you have learned, they were not exactly upscale. So perhaps it was Dad's self-respect as breadwinner for his family that Mom would have hurt if she had said she wanted to look for work.

Then there were "the girls." Although she socialized easily and graciously with neighbors, church members, and the parents of our school friends, Mom's oldest and best friends were the members of her Bridge Club, some of whom had started first grade with her at Columbus School for Girls in 1916 and gone right through with her to high school graduation in 1928. "The girls" had crazy-sounding nicknames—Toppie, Postie, Miggs—but nearly all of them were first the daughters and later the husbands of rich, conservative Columbus professional men and business leaders. In their ideological underpinnings, they had much in common with the East Coast clubwomen of Helen E. Hokinson's famous *New Yorker* cartoons, and some of the more arch, though certainly not the more Bohemian, personalities in Mary McCarthy's *The Group*. Their politics—and my parents' also— were extremely conservative. In 1952, I remember, Mom and Dad loved to tell their friends that they were members of the 4-H Club: "Help Hurry Harry Home!"—Harry being, of course, then-President Truman. And in the Republican primary that year, they voted for Ohio Senator Bob Taft because they thought that General Eisenhower was too liberal. In this they reflected the vast majority of the people I knew at the time. There were only about three Democratic families in Upper Arlington in the fifties, and although it was not often discussed openly, we all knew who they were. As I'm sure was true of many of my classmates, my home training taught me to regard them with suspicion. Columbus then was as segregated, both as to race and class, as any Southern town I could imagine after years of living in North Carolina, so the political opinions of working-class people and people of color flew far beneath the prevailing Republican radar. Dad used to come home from the office with stories of how his secretary said she could spot Democrats because their eyes were set narrowly in their foreheads, giving them a furtive, or in extreme cases even a cross-eyed, look. But by the time I was a teenager I began to realize, in spite of all this indoctrination, that Democrats seemed to enjoy life more than Republicans, if only because GOP conservatism and repression stifled imagination and gave Democrats a lot to laugh about.

Bridge Club, that bastion of the Old Order, met every month, and it was a major event when it was Mom's turn—especially since she did not have the options that some of the other "girls" did, either of having it at the country club or of having it catered at their homes. Most of them lived across town in Bexley, the "old money" suburb, whereas with only a couple of other families, we lived in Upper Arlington, the "new money" suburb. Actually, as far as we were concerned, it was the "no money" suburb, for we simply could not compete economically with the rest of Bridge Club. Although they were her dearest friends, I think that Mom felt a little under the gun when they came to our house. The Bexley "girls" had to be made to feel that it was worth their trouble to drive all the way downtown and then out the other side; there were no freeways yet, and even after there were, it took most of "the girls" years to know how to use them, and still longer to deem them acceptable. There was always a thorough housecleaning, a meticulous polishing of silver, an ironing of linen tablecloths and napkins for the table and of dainty monogrammed hand towels for the bathroom, and a great deal of very serious cooking going on in the hours leading up to Bridge Club at our house.

I used to be intimidated by "the girls." I sensed from my mother's behavior that they could pull rank on us—though, to be fair, they never did, for they truly loved Mom and the girlhood memories they shared. The husbands were mostly as stuffy as they were rich, except for one who could wiggle his ears, and one who was, like my father, a musician and a reader. I wonder now just how Dad managed it on the occasions when the husbands joined the wives and they all socialized together. I surmise that it was the men's patronizing of my poorer but far more creative father, rather than any slights towards Mom, that did damage to self-esteem, if indeed any damage was done. But the women were a different story— partly because Dad was handsome and clever, partly because they may have felt a kind of excitement at our house that was missing in their larger, more elegant, but more placid homes. As I got older and they got older, I realized that many of them were kind, generous, and fun to talk to. On a beautiful sunny, breezy summer day while Dad was at work, we went on an expedition with one "girl," Ruth Young, who drove us in her huge Pontiac "woodie" station wagon to her family's farm northwest of Columbus. With gusto she gave us a short tour, and we went exploring in the fields and picked zucchini while Mom and her friend, whom she called "Ruthie," sat in the shade and talked for hours. Still alive and alert well into her nineties, Ruth stayed in touch with Molly and wrote me in 2005 to say how much she had always loved and admired both Mom and Dad for their brains and wit. Ruth died in the summer of 2009, surely the last of Bridge Club to go; she was 100 years old. During the year I was an English-language assistant in Bordeaux, another "girl," Lib Saxby, on vacation in France with her husband and daughter, got in touch with me and took me out to dinner. I cried when I heard her voice on the hotel phone—the first Ohio voice I had heard in eight months. Mom had always told us how lucky we were to be born in the Middle West, where there was no regional accent to stop our upward progress in the world. I learned that day that she was wrong.

Yet another "girl" told the best funny stories. Martha (Mart) Kirsten once regaled Mom with the tale of a fender-bender she got into while out shopping on a Saturday morning. What was funny, as Mart herself realized, was what worried her about it. Instead of feeling lucky that she had escaped serious injury in the wreck, all she could think about was how embarrassed she had been in the emergency room because she hadn't showered that morning before going out. Not only that, but all the nurses could see that she was wearing her old underwear, which was full of holes. Then, Mom said, she roared with laughter in her rich baritone and took another puff on her cigarette.

Mart was Mom's equal in wit and spirit; it was she who had had the nerve to marry the only musical-literary Bridge Club husband other than Dad. Not long after attending Molly's wedding, strapped to an oxygen tank, she died of emphysema—the tragic result of all those cigarettes. We all mourned her premature departure, remembering how much she loved Mom and how often she had made us laugh.

The definitive Bridge Club moment occurred during an evening gathering of "the girls" and their husbands at our house. I need to explain that as they all got older, less and less bridge was played while more and more liquor was consumed. The living room was filled with men and women, cigarette smoke, and ever louder and more energetic conversation. I was away, perhaps at college, and didn't witness the mythic confrontation I am about to relate. Dad and Mom were mingling with the guests. Molly and Fred had been banished to the kitchen, but the sliding door into the living room was open.

It was Molly who later reported that two of "the girls," forced by the limited seating in our living room to share the piano bench, had become involved in a heated discussion. Their body language as they turned, gaped, reared, and brayed at each other threatened the equilibrium of their narrow perch, but owing to the general din, Molly could not make out what they were saying. Then suddenly the room fell almost silent, as when the French say an angel is passing. This is what Molly heard—but it was not angelic:

> "GIRL" #1: "Sweetbreads and brains are the same thing!"—spit out with the acute, infuriated indignation usually reserved to challenge any infidel's claim that the King James Bible was anything but the direct, verbatim, and unmediated word of God.

> "GIRL" #2: "They are not!"—declaimed in a tone of high Yankee dudgeon appropriate for correcting someone dumb enough to question whether Lincoln had freed the slaves.

At that moment, the other guests resumed their impenetrable babble, and my sister never learned how the organ-meat discussion progressed beyond that point.

Chuckling inside, I half-returned to the present reality of the Pyramid Point trail, still thinking about Mom, bears and birds, visiting spirits, nice eggs, and Bridge Club. Our sighting of the indigo bunting wasn't the first time since my rediscovery of Leelanau that I had asked myself questions about bird ghosts. Two years previously, I had stopped along M-22 just north of Port Oneida to photograph a melancholy-looking birch swamp that lies right by the highway. I walked along the road until I came to a small bridge over the water, when the sound of my steps startled a blue heron below me in the tall grasses. I heard first a loud snapping noise and then the rush of the great wings as the magnificent creature rose up and flew away. Shaken physically and emotionally, I remembered then, as I recall now, that Mom had been fascinated by these birds. Indeed she had proudly shown us one while Dad was rowing us down the Platte River years ago. Was she the bird, or was she somehow in the bird? Like it, like a bear, she was big, powerful, capable of both awkwardness and grace. And I know she would have loved to rise up like the heron out of the marsh—sudden, stern, loud, majestic in strength.

The year we all saw the heron, Dad had rented us a rowboat at the Platte River boat livery, several miles south of Empire in Benzie County, and we were partly rowing but mostly drifting our way down the shallow but swift-running Platte towards the big lake. Though Dad did most of it, Fred and I took turns rowing or guiding, keeping an eye out for rocks or branches that we might hit with the boat, but watching also for signs of the abundant wildlife of this area.

Mom eagerly eyed the river and its banks, immediately able to identify nearly every strange plant or animal we saw. There were frogs and turtles sunning on rocks and logs, fish darting through the water, and a variety of water birds nesting in the marshes. Then she spied the heron, motionless but regal in the shadows. We knew immediately that this was a major sighting, because instead of shouting at us, she whispered. Shortly we all were staring slack-jawed, breathless. Then, as suddenly as Mom first saw it, the bird, reacting to our presence on the water, rose with a loud clatter and flew quickly out of sight. Recalling it now, I think that an angel's wings would have to make the same sound. No one spoke for a minute or two as we continued our downstream journey.

We eventually came to the beach where the Platte runs out into the big lake. We pulled up the boat so it wouldn't drift away, got out the picnic we had brought, walked across the sand to be closer to the lake, and then settled down to have lunch. After that, we sunbathed, swam, read, or played cards until three o'clock, when a man from the marina office arrived in a boat with a powerful outboard motor to haul our boat and any other drifting rowboats back up to the docks, where we had left our car. Dad waded out into the water to help him attach our boat to the towboat. We still have a photo, taken during my high school years, of all five of us and Mickey at the Platte River beach. We are sitting literally like bumps on a log—a huge driftwood log that we found there. All of us, including Mickey, look happy. When Fred, Molly, and I revisited the Platte in 2002 with all of our children, we found a similar log and got one of the younger generation—I think it was Fred and Liz's daughter Marian—to take our picture on it.

Day travelers down the Platte today do not get towed back up to the office. Instead, before the rowing tour begins, visitors drive their vehicles down to the beach parking lot, leave them, and are brought back to the starting place by office employees in vans. That way, once you get all the way down the river to the beach, you can get into your car and leave any time you wish, but you miss the return trip back up the river. This is a plus for those on tight schedules, but a disappointment if you want to take another look at the vegetation—or search for herons.

Now, Fred and I walked on through the woods and up the increasingly steep trail to the lookout at Pyramid Point. Because of the increasing cloud cover, the view over the water was disappointingly limited. The blue-gray haze that makes long views impossible brought into relief the wind-twisted shapes of the trees growing between us and the drop-off, their naked roots partly exposed by the relentless forces of wind, rain, and snow. Fred laughed wryly at a warning sign erected near the cliff, apparently the product of a Lakeshore bureaucracy that mandates certain sign standards—number of attaching screws, type of protective cover—whether they are needed or not. But I felt closed in, depressed a little by the haze, and began to think gloomily that my brother and I were like the old trees in front of us, highlighted in the grotesqueness of our aging against the abyss of time and mortality that confronted us. But simultaneously I was enlivened, rejuvenated by the motion of the hike itself, and even more by the mere possibility that my mother's blue eyes had winked at us in the bunting's splendid feathers. We turned back down from the overlook and chose a path that would take us through the forest to a wide meadow and then back again to the forest. By the time the rain began, we were under thick tree-cover and heard rather than felt it as it fell. The Leelanau green world around us seemed kindly, safe, and only a little bit weird as we hiked back to the trailhead.

On a hot, bright afternoon later that same summer, I drove alone to stops 9 and 10 on the Pierce Stocking Scenic Drive, which winds over the Sleeping Bear dunes. The parking lot at these stops was crowded, as is usual for July: it is from here that tourists like to descend the dangerously steep western face of the dunes all the way to the big lake. The National Park Service discourages this: sternly worded signs warn of the danger of landslides and the strenuousness of the return climb, which is even steeper than at the official climbing face on M-109. Still, the rangers do not absolutely forbid it, and on this sun-drenched afternoon, with the big lake so splendidly blue, I saw many children and quite a few adults perched or climbing on the golden slope, some as far down as the water line hundreds of feet below.

My own mission for this day, like theirs, was one that is officially discouraged. I planned to walk across the dunes, where there is no path to follow, in order to visit the Sleeping Bear pinnacle dune, the one that has given the entire Lakeshore its name. Seeing the rise and the blowout up close, I had decided, would somehow put me in closer touch with my mother. Anne-Marie Oomen's essay and her personal example of braving the dunes in midwinter had convinced me that I must make this trek.

I walked out to a raised observation platform to get my bearings. Affixed to the railing, in the line of sight towards the pinnacle, was a small identifying picture and brief legend. From here the rise was just a small blip on the horizon. I saw the direction I should take. It seemed easy enough except for a wooded declivity, about a third of the way to the pinnacle, that I would have to negotiate.

As passionate as she was about so many things, my mother rarely acted on impulse. In fact she brought us up to follow the rules—to be good, obedient citizens—with frequent exhortations that covered everything from bicycle safety to being polite to strangers. So it felt odd, even wrong to me to throw first one leg and then the other over the platform railing and into the pathless sand in what suddenly seemed a self-important, even harebrained way of paying her homage. Superego kicked in, and I both feared and actually expected that other tourists who saw what I was doing would cry out against my transgression and order me back to the path. But of course no one paid me any mind at all, and I made my way steadily out onto the dunes. Once away from the others and their noise, I felt my mind expanding into the marvelous quiet of the dunes on that perfect summer afternoon. I was alone with the brilliance of the sunlight that danced on the hot sand under my feet and the cold blue water far below. All I could hear now was the wind. It spoke in two voices, both of them gentle today: one rising from the lake, echoing the vastness of water and sky; and another, closer by, more intimate, that ruffled the dune vegetation as I passed.

As I approached the split in the dunes, I looked down and saw it was deep and thickly wooded. I decided to turn inland from the lake, assuming that if I went far enough, the cut would grow shallower. But just the opposite was true: it was actually growing deeper, and almost before I realized it, I found myself dangerously close to the edge of what had become a steep drop-off. Just then, I heard from below a loud, crackling noise that could only have been made by a large animal, startled at my presence, moving suddenly in the woods below. Probably a deer, I thought; but I couldn't help remembering that one of the Lakeshore rangers I had recently interviewed spoke of a recent Michigan Wildlife project of studying cougar scats found on the dunes.

The potential for confrontation with a cougar immediately banished any remaining temptation to cross the split by descending into it. Nor, it seemed, could I get around it on the inland side without making a long, time-consuming detour. So I turned in my tracks and headed towards the lake. To my relief, I soon saw that my first surmise was wrong: near the steep lakeside drop-off, I could easily bypass the split and continue on my journey towards the pinnacle.

Now that I could walk with more assurance of reaching my goal, I noticed more closely the delicate grasses near me on the sand, the dazzling sun on the lake far below me, and an ore freighter making its slow but steady way across the bunting-blue water. On my right, I passed a vertical wall of sand taller than I am, which the wind had engraved with hieroglyphics not unlike those I have so often seen carved on the stones at Empire Beach. As with the stones, I wished I could read this text; I wondered whether it could tell me things I don't know or don't remember about my mother and father and our long-ago early lives. I kept thinking I was about to reach the pinnacle, but every time I came up a small rise and thought it would be just before me, I saw there was another little valley to walk through.

Finally I arrived. Coming to the Sleeping Bear Pinnacle from the south as I did, I saw to the right, inland from the lake, the still wooded cusp that marks its eastern boundary; to my left was the vast boneyard of dead trees. The ancient trunks and branches assumed odd, even grotesque shapes. Some lay collapsed, apparently exhausted, on the sand, as if exposure to the light had wakened them only to let them die a second time. Some, twisted eons ago, now seemed coiled tense with animal life, ready to strike. Still others— once pine trunks, long, tapering, straight, like those Deje and I had seen two years before on the Sleeping Bear Point trail—protruded from the cusp and hillocks at angles that transcended the limits of both gravity and imagination. One amazing fifteen-foot-long pointed spike stretched parallel to the ground but six feet above it, its root end still held in a small rise in the sand. It was completely counter-intuitive to see the heavy log so amazingly suspended over the dune floor, and after snapping a photo, I stood and watched it for several minutes to see whether it would collapse and fall. It didn't.

Whether one reads in these images the potential for renewed life, or only death and decay grossly prolonged, it was easy once again to see why the Lakeshore refers to such places as "ghost forests." I saw my mother's bones imaged in these silvery logs, both the straight and the twisted. I seemed also to see into her brain, into the detritus of her hopes, fears, accomplishments, and unfulfilled desires. But was it my mother's unconscious that the blowout revealed—or, since my own imagination had become so kindled by the sight, mine? Here, alone in the exposed womb of the Sleeping Bear Pinnacle, I continued to explore my feelings. I began to think I had come on a pilgrimage both holy and profane, much like Chaucer's medieval pilgrims as they traveled towards Canterbury. In the geographic and mythic center of the Ojibwa narrative of maternal love and pain, I would find some sense of continuing connection with my mother.

With my back to the sun and the lake, and my face turned toward what was left of the partly forested pinnacle, I began to talk to her, slowly, calmly, easily. I told her I had walked out there on the dunes in search of her. I told her what a wonderful mother I think she was; how well she poured her great energy into her many activities; what a fine role model she was in her cooking, her ceramics, her gardening, her sewing and needlework, her constant reading, her desire always to know more about the natural world, her love of a good time. I told her that given all her power and abilities, I understood better now both what she gained and what she gave up in order to be such a superparent. I told her that we all remembered her every day by cooking from her recipes, eating off the dishes she made for us, pursuing her interest in nature, using her turns of phrase, or pausing on the way upstairs to see the intricacy of her needlework hanging framed on the landing. I told her I had started to write about her and Dad and our Glen Lake vacations because we were all so happy then. I told her I have had a rewarding career as a professor, a mutually nourishing marriage, and three wonderful children. I said that while I might not have accomplished everything she thought me capable of, still I felt I had accomplished much of value, and I was not unhappy with my life.

Now come to the end of this one-man memorial service, I felt that in the quiet of the pinnacle, broken only by the wind, with the sun still pouring light and life down on the earth, I was holding my life safe and whole. The day was so beautiful that the starkness of the ghost trees could only fascinate, not depress me. I couldn't feel downcast, but I knew that however much I had wanted it and made room for it by coming to the pinnacle, there had been no transcendence, no real vision. I had gone for my walk, taken my pictures, spoken my piece to Mom in a place that itself seemed both a source of new life and a graveyard of lost dreams. I was full to the brim with my life and hers—but it had not picked me up, moved me, taken me further: no ghost had answered. Perhaps, two years after her death, I had passed beyond the grief and pain of her dying to a new place of easier, less painful intimacy. Perhaps it was not only psychologically but morally wrong to seek deliberately to have such an experience. I felt content with my hike, but at the same time chastened, almost rebuked.

The last time I saw my mother alive was a terrible day both outside and in. It was mid-December in Cincinnati, where Fred and his family live. The sun was invisible, almost unimaginable, beyond the leaden vault of the sky, and a puny but treacherous wet snow was falling numbly, stupidly, on top of the filthy, pockmarked snow already on the ground. Rutted, iced-over slush coated the parking lot of the retirement center, and it was all I could do to get from my car to the entrance without tumbling into the half-frozen mess. Inside, the overheated lobby was bright with twinkling holiday decorations, piped-in music, and even a real fire in a real fireplace. I walked straight to the elevator.

Upstairs, in the room we tried to make cheerful for her with her pictures and books, Mom was slowly dying. Fred, who had arrived earlier, led me to her bedside. She lay inert, sunk irretrievably now into the depression and dementia that already for several years had made her first a different person and then a non-person. For a while after Dad died, we could, by teasing her, rouse her into some semblance of her earlier high-spirited, fractious self. One of us would tell her he had eaten all her Hershey bars—she had become addicted to them—or that he wanted her to cook us a "nice egg." She knew the drill, knew what we wanted her to say, and she could just manage to get out the right words: "Well, get me some more then," or "Cook it yourself!" "No back talk!" and "Pipe down!" were no longer in her repertory, and in her eyes I could see that she didn't have the heart anymore; she may even have resented being asked. Instead—and this really threw us at first—she actually became sweet and nice. This may have been a result of her dementia, but it also seemed just barely possible that she had consciously adopted the dear-little-old-lady persona in order to get back at Fred and me. In any case, it was strangely unsettling. We were left waiting for the other shoe to fall, even as it became increasingly apparent that there would be no more shoes falling.

While she was still able to get about, Deje and I would take her out for dinner during our visits; but increasingly, she took little interest in either her food or her surroundings. And in fact it was her complete rejection of nourishment, which had begun two months previously, that was killing her now. Fred, Molly, and I had decided that it would be wrong to try to keep Mom alive by intravenous feeding or other artificial means; whatever was robbing her appetite, it seemed that this was the point at which we needed to let her go. Fred had already had a priest from his Episcopal church come to administer last rites. Amazingly, he reported, in view of her longstanding prejudice against anything that seemed even remotely Catholic, Mom seemed both to understand what was happening and to accept it.

As nearly extinguished as she was, still it was agonizing to say goodbye to her. Fred was there with me in the room. The bed faced a window, where earlier she had liked to look out and watch for birds, so I tried to get her to open her eyes to look outside. In fact I lied and said the snow that was falling was fresh and beautiful. I will never know for sure whether she couldn't hear or make sense of what I was saying, or whether she could tell I was lying and refused to respond to such hypocrisy. Nothing I could think of to say roused her. Although she lived nearly a month longer, she was already too far gone, and what was left was not her, not the magnificent and sometimes terrifying woman I had known.

In despair, I kissed her, said "Goodbye, dear," and then bolted from the room almost without saying goodbye to Fred. I was sobbing as I again crossed the icy parking lot, robbed, as it seemed then, not only of a deathbed blessing, but of any chance of formal closure. My effort to break through to her had failed, and in any case I had to hit the road, drive to Kenyon College where our younger son Jamie was then a junior, and pick up him and his gear to take him home to North Carolina for the Christmas break. Mom died ten days into the new year.

At her funeral, Fred and Liz's priest, a woman, frankly and humorously acknowledged that she knew our mother would most likely not have approved of female clergy or a good many other things about the early twenty-first century. Our cousin Sam McGavran, a naval officer retired after a distinguished career, had brought his sister Jane down from Columbus for the service, even though he was already sick with the cancer that would kill him before the year was over. He joked with us about how Episcopalians say, "Forgive us our trespasses," instead of the Presbyterian "our debts" we all had learned as children. We all sang the familiar funeral hymn "Our God, Our Help in Ages Past" and "I Am the Bread of Life," a new-fangled one that Mom wouldn't have known and couldn't have liked. Still, I teared up each time we came to the refrain: "And I will raise them up on the last day."

Looking back now, I find much selfishness in my extravagant expectations and equally extravagant grief. Who was I to assume that my presence would magically resuscitate her? Or that she would say some hugely significant thing to me at the end—not of her life, but of my brief visit? In any case, dementia, or its close relative Alzheimer's disease, regularly leads more and more of us to farewell scenes like this one. My last real opportunity to say goodbye to Mom had come and gone several years before; but how could I have known? how can anyone know the right moment and seize it? We have already started missing the people we love, almost imperceptibly at first, and when we finally realize it, they aren't there anymore—it's too late.

But I have also come to think it is wrong to "seek closure," as the talk-show psychologists call it, for the loss of the persons we love the most. Surely we don't want to *forget* the beloved one. Besides, dramatic deathbed moments seem more the province of the movies than of real life; some actors—one thinks of Debra Winger—seem to specialize in portentous onscreen dying. Writing these words now doesn't bring me closer to closure, whatever that is, but I find that by trying to write my mother's life—including her dying—through my Leelanau memories, I feel her alive in me to a degree I couldn't begin to imagine on that gray day when I left her bedside for the last time.

Then something weird, almost shocking, occurs: I realize that I couldn't find my mother at the pinnacle blowout because I had already found her in the deep crevice in the dunes that I had been obliged to avoid in my hike. That deep split had attracted my notice even before I left the observation platform, and I had been torn by opposing instincts as I approached it. Part of me wanted to descend, even lose my balance and fall, deep into the thick vegetation; but then there was that ominous animal sound I heard lurking in the depths. Now I see that my moment of enlightenment—and, since I had repressed it, a tritely oedipal one—occurred before I got to the pinnacle with its remnant of forest and its grotesque shapes. Sure enough, I had found my sleeping mother, both desired and terrifying, in the Sleeping Bear. And as I write these words, Dr. Freud express-mails me another letter bomb: I remember the only time I ever saw my mother naked.

I was probably fifteen. I was looking for something in my parents' bedroom. (Yes, I really was, I don't remember what—but I can hardly make myself write that incredibly disingenuous line.) I knew it was the time of the afternoon when my mother usually "got cleaned up," as she used to say, for Dad's arrival home at dinnertime; but I persuaded myself that since I hadn't heard any water running, she must still be downstairs in the kitchen. Then the bathroom door opened and she stepped out from the shower, completely bare. It was the primal scene, all right. Hamlet's confrontation with Gertrude in her bedchamber, after "The Mousetrap," pales by comparison. But unlike Hamlet, I had no great sins to lay at her feet, no tricks to catch the conscience of the queen. There was only my imperfect adolescent love, my blindness to her love and pain, and all my rude, eggy litanies of teasing. Neither of us expected to see the other. Yet it was as if she had been rehearsing this scene for years. Had I been, too? Not consciously, that's for sure; I stood staring, transfixed. With neither anger nor tears, she strolled easily across the room to her dresser and got out some clean underwear. Then, and only then, she said very kindly that I had better leave the room. In my memory, my mother will always remain as she was that day: powerful yet vulnerable, totally exposed yet revealing nothing— finally elusive, mysterious, and, in spite of everything I have told you, unknowable.

Here we all are at the Platte River Beach on Lake Michigan in 1957: Dad, Mom, me, Fred, Molly, and Mickey.

Mom and Dad relax with manhattans at Salisbury Beach on Little
Glen Lake, 1955. The Ritz is in the background, behind Dad.

The 1952 Ford Ranch Wagon parked at the back door of The Ritz, early 1950s.

Dad plays the sun down on his accordion at one of our Empire
Beach picnics, early 1950s.

Fred, me, and Molly sitting on Salisbury Dock, Little Glen Lake, in the late afternoon sun, early 1950s. That's the Alligator behind us.

Less than a year after they were married in 1936, Mom and Dad took a day trip to Castalia, Ohio, to visit the Blue Hole.

Here is Dad at the Blue Hole in 1937. He and Mom got all dressed up like movie stars for a long, hot car trip to see a natural wonder.

Mom strikes a classic pin-up pose on the Sleeping Bear Sand Dune, 1949.

Dad brings to the Sleeping Bear Dune climb, in the early 1950s, some of the élan with which he attacked the bat in the bedroom several years earlier.

I'm probably seventeen here as I perform the ritual climbing of Mishimokwa, the Sleeping Bear, late 1950s.

This is the unforgettable moment when Mom put on her 1926 flapper dress and did the Charleston for us in our living room in Columbus before going out to a party with Dad, mid 1950s.

Mom descends Sleeping Bear in her famous Gina Lollobrigida shirt, mid 1950s.

Andrew Horning and Catherine McGavran share a laugh on their wedding day, June 18, 2005, Suttons Bay. Photo is used courtesy of Gary L. Howe.

Mark and Jamie escort Deje at Catherine and Andrew's wedding.

Here I am escorting Catherine at her wedding to Andrew Horning.

Here are all the current-generation McGavrans at our big Leelanau reunion in 2002. *Front row*: Liz McGavran, Deje McGavran, John Crabb, Molly Crabb, Catherine McGavran. *Back row*: Marian McGavran, Fred McGavran, Sarah McGavran, Rebecca Crabb, David Crabb, Fred Crabb, Mark McGavran, Jamie McGavran, and me.

This is me, little Jimmy, with Mom and Dad on top of the Sleeping Bear in 1949, our first trip to Leelanau.

PART THREE

SHADOWS OF DAD

The suitcases and the playpen, the Frisbees and the Wiffle Balls are all packed in the wayback of the car; the snacks are on the floor of the front seat where Deje can dole them out to our hungry kids as we drive south towards Charlotte. I go back inside Mom and Dad's house in Columbus for the farewell ritual. We stand around smiling nervously for a moment; then thank-yous, handshaking, and hugging begin—and a few tears. Dad waits till he hears the first sniffles; then he says, "You know we can't miss you 'til you're gone." A stranger overhearing this might brand him a cross old misanthrope who can't wait to get rid of his noisy grandchildren and settle down again to his typewriter or a good book. But we know him, and these words actually send us laughing out the door. He has just told us two things: (1) Get into the car, you need to hit the road; and (2) Mom and I will feel lonely as soon as you do that. As I write this now, Dad's words turn around in my brain: "Now *you* are gone, and I miss you every day." When Deje quoted his farewell line at the funeral home after his death, we all immediately burst into tears. But I haven't always understood all my father's ironies as clearly as I have this one.

In July 2004, three years after we found The Ritz, Deje and I were back in Leelanau with my sister, who had flown from her home in Alberta to spend a few days with us. One afternoon Molly and I went on a mission to Empire Beach. As we walked by the water, we searched the sand for the heart-shaped stones that we remembered from childhood. We were collecting them to use as table decorations at Cathy's wedding, which was scheduled for the following June in Suttons Bay. We stooped from time to time to pick up stones and turn them in our hands, noting their form and color. If they measured up to our high standards, we kept them.

It was a mild, sunny day, and sunbathers, swimmers, and picnickers were scattered in small groups across the beach. Suddenly a woman rose from a faded beach towel. She strode in front of us across the sand and walked straight into the water. She seemed to be chasing a preteenage girl who was already jumping in the waves. It must have been her daughter, but she wasn't scolding her or calling her back. The woman was short and overweight, her swimsuit hard-tasked to contain her, her black hair tied back in a severe ponytail. But in a moment the big lake transformed her: she was as light and quick as a girl again in the shock of the cold water and the joy of playing with her child. They looked full into each other's faces, laughing and chatting. Then the woman dove like a porpoise into the next wave; her daughter squealed excitedly and followed her. When they came up, they were in each other's arms, laughing again. As I walked on with Molly, I probably missed several good heart-stones because I kept glancing over my shoulder at the two of them.

Not everyone there that day was laughing. Earlier, while I was parking, the car in the space next to mine caught my eye. The big old Mercury sedan wore a layer of dirt so thick I hardly could tell what color it was painted—something pale and bland

and tired-looking, beige perhaps. It was covered with scratches, dents, and dings that bespoke a long lifetime of minor indignities and occasional major assaults; and a lacy rust two-tone around the wheel openings proved it had endured many Michigan winters. Then, just as I was getting out of my car, I realized that the Mercury was not empty. Once over my initial shock—I had dropped back onto the seat—I looked again at the man who sat motionless behind the wheel. He was pale, bespectacled, fleshy but not obese, of no particular age. On his head was a fake-fleece winter cap with tied-up earflaps that gave him a vaguely military aspect. The windows were all rolled up in spite of the July heat, and there he sat, motionless, staring out past the beach towards the water. What was he looking for? I couldn't know, but often I too look out over the big lake, across the years, scanning the horizons of memory. I closed my car door as softly as I could and went to find Molly on the beach.

I was preoccupied, as I had been with each return to Empire Beach since 2001: Was it my memory or the contours of this place that had changed in half a century? I still couldn't decide where Dad used to stand when he played his accordion at our beach picnics—and I couldn't locate Dad in my mind either. Images of my mother had risen quickly, even irrepressibly, since my return to Leelanau. It was different with Dad: I had to dive deeper and, as with the heart-stones, search more closely. He was everywhere and nowhere, present but elusive—as if in Mom's shadow. He was never a soldier, but in my mind he had gone missing in action.

It had also affected my willingness to play his instrument. For the last three summers, I had brought the ancient Hohner with us to Leelanau. Miraculously, it still played—as loud, wheezy, and cheerful as ever. In the time since Dad passed it on to me, I had had all the straps replaced—the big over-the-shoulder straps, the smaller left-hand strap, the tiny closing straps that hold it together on the closet shelf at home. It had seen me through several gigs over the years as strolling entertainer, party-stopping noisemaker, and gypsy-orchestra-pit musician, but the bellows seemed sound. The instrument was not the problem.

When push came to shove—as it always does with an accordion—I hadn't had the heart to play it. I knew the old songs Dad played on those August evenings long ago, and when pressed by Fred or Molly, I had done it—but it hadn't felt right. When I played it in Summer 2002, at the Leelanau family reunion Fred, Molly, and I had with all our children, I wept— sentimentally at first, and then angrily, disgusted with my own weak-minded confusion. As I write these words, I realize that my diffidence about playing Dad's accordion, like my worry about where he stood when he played it, has been clouding all my recollections of my father.

Who was he? Editor, writer, amateur musician, maker of manhattans and funny quips? All these things I knew about him, but they didn't really answer the question. He probably spent more time with us than most other fathers did with their kids in the forties and fifties, but that still wasn't a whole lot of time. His job as writer and managing editor of a small, syndicated home magazine kept him busy at his office every weekday. His only official vacation time, apart from national holidays, was the two weeks we spent at Glen Lake. And his ambition to break into the wider world of professional publishing sent him many evenings to our basement, to an old typewriter on an old desk, where he wrote and rewrote his essays and stories.

That was OK when we were little, since he put us to bed before he began to write. We missed him more as we grew older: our paths didn't cross as much, as our own evenings were increasingly taken up with homework, extracurricular activities, and socializing. Weekends, of course, we saw more of him. There were always Saturday chores—dandelions to pull, grass to cut, leaves to rake, snow to shovel—often with him. And sometimes he would take me with him down West Fifth Avenue for his regular Saturday stops at the Ohio Wine Store and Swan Cleaners. Sundays we all went to Boulevard Presbyterian Church, but except for the time in the car going and coming back, there was little time for talk. And even then, Mom and Dad mostly chatted with each other in the front seat. It was fun to eavesdrop on them since often they compared notes regarding other church members, and their remarks tended to focus on things like mid-sermon gas attacks and halitosis blasts during hymn-singing. But it wasn't the same as talking with Dad.

On the beach at Empire, I shared these frustrations with Molly. She told me that one of the reasons she loved Leelanau so much as a girl was that Dad was there all the time for us for those two weeks. As with everything else Molly says, this made excellent sense—yet I don't remember feeling this way myself. In my mind he seemed to fade into the background even at Little Glen—except, of course, when he played the Hohner, which could serve as a background instrument only in a hurricane. Anyway, you can't talk to a man playing an accordion without risking permanent ear or vocal-chord damage.

Like many other men of his generation, Dad was not physically demonstrative. I was told this very early, but did not realize for decades what it meant, or what effect even the telling of it could have on me. In what must be one of my first clear visual and verbal memories—I couldn't have been more than four—I was sitting on the kitchen-door steps of our house with Mom and my little brother Fred. Dad was at work, and Molly had not yet been born.

It was a bright morning; perhaps we were about to walk down the street to a small neighborhood market for a few groceries, or up the alley behind our house to visit a neighbor, an older woman Mom enjoyed chatting with. In summer, Frances had beautiful hollyhocks by her garage that were taller than I was.

I don't remember where we went that day, nor do I recall how the topic arose, but I will never forget what Mom said to us as we sat there on the steps: "You know, boys, Daddy loves you very much—even though he may not always show it." She was crying softly by the time she finished. I was, as I said, very young, but not too young to be amazed: it was the first time I had seen my tall, strong, beautiful mother cry. And it had never occurred to me to wonder whether my father loved us. Mom might have been responding to something one of us had just said, or to something Dad had done—or failed to do—with us the previous evening. Or it could have been some private worry that had nothing to do with us. Whatever the explanation, she must have believed that Fred and I would have benefited from more contact with Dad. As I pondered it now, I wondered whether, as we grew older, some of Dad's interactions with us were things that she had contrived. I wondered too whether Mom's sad words so long ago could have unintentionally planted in me the idea that I was missing Dad. In my current depression I thought cynically that I had always missed him, in more ways than one.

Molly and I turned to continue our search for heart-rocks by doubling back on our steps, this time a little further from the edge of the lake. Ahead I saw the mother-daughter swimmers out of the water now, resting on their towels on the sand. I told Molly my memory of Mom's early distress. In response, she shared something that Mom told her many years later. Molly and John were visiting in Columbus with their children, and she and Mom were looking out a kitchen window at Dad, who was playing in the backyard with the kids. Mom watched Dad for a minute and then said, "I never could have predicted this." And it was true. If Dad had been shy about showing affection for us when we were young, he did a 180-degree turnaround and became a doting, involved grandfather with all of our children. And through loving his grandchildren more openly, he found it easier to share affection with us as well. It worked both ways, too: as he grew older, it became possible for me not just to shake hands with him, but to hug him at the beginning and end of a visit home.

I was discouraged as I walked with Molly at Empire Beach that afternoon. But now, as I write, I realize that I had allowed my small uncertainty about the Hohner dune, and larger uncertainties about male preoccupations and male intimacy, to block all my recollections of Dad. It no longer mattered where he stood with his accordion. He was there, he played it, and in doing so he revealed much of himself: his art, his generosity, and his diffidence and detachment as well. Memories race into my consciousness now; I am impatient to set them down. With the breakup of my mental logjam comes another revelation, this time in the form of a question: Did I struggle to remember Dad because Mom eclipsed him in my brain, because I felt truly estranged from him, or because over time I have become so much like him that I can no longer differentiate us? Writer, editor, amateur musician? All those tags describe me too—but I needed my sister's calm voice to understand it.

It was August, sometime in the fifties, and we were about to leave Little Glen for Empire and another of our epic beach picnics. I was reading in the living room of the cottage, and Dad was in the kitchen making manhattans—a whole thermos full of them, since they were the mixed drink of choice for my parents and many of their friends. I heard him say something like "m-m-m"; he must have been tasting them to see if they needed more vermouth or Angostura bitters. He started to carry the thermos out of the kitchen—I heard his steps coming towards me. Then there was a terrible crash as the thermos handle broke off in his hand, the bottle hit the floor, and a quart of manhattans poured out across the ancient, sand-scarred linoleum. Their rich, sweet aroma soon filled the small cottage. Dad did not yell or curse at this dreadful turn of events; he simply said "Oh, no," in the tone Thoreau no doubt had in mind when he wrote of quiet desperation. I heard him mutter to himself that he did not have enough whiskey or vermouth to mix another batch. Then one of his friends, as if drawn by the odor wafting out towards Little Glen, strode into the kitchen, assessed the situation, and joked with Dad about getting down on their hands and knees and lapping up the precious liquid. I don't know what Mom and Dad and the others drank that night on the beach; they probably bought beer at the Friendly Tavern.

The scene has shifted, and I see him playing his accordion. The last rays of the setting sun gild his tanned skin, the fingers of his right hand fly over the keys, those of his left find the accompanying bass and chord buttons, and his arms alternately squeeze and open again in order to maintain the airflow through the bellows. We kids run on the beach, talking and laughing, and keep watch for a sunset freighter. We hear the adults singing loudly, nostalgically, to Dad's playing: "With someone like you, a pal good and true . . . we'll find perfect peace, where joys never cease, and let the rest of the world go by." But Dad himself is not singing; this is partly because he is concentrating on playing, partly because in spite of his musical talent, he doesn't sing well. But his silence at the heart of his music also suggests that my elusive father has withdrawn from the scene he himself has created.

He didn't always withdraw, I reflect. Now it's bedtime at home in Columbus. I sit in the bathtub behind Fred. This had to have happened in the forties when we were still small enough to fit into the tub together. It's hot and steamy in the small bathroom, and Dad is bathing us. He has taken off his tie and rolled up the sleeves of the white shirt he wore to work. On his knees, he leans over the tub. He washes our faces and rinses them quickly, before the soap can get into our eyes and sting. We take turns sliding the slippery bar of Kirk's Castile over ourselves. This always makes us giggle. Still laughing, we pass it to Dad so he can wash our backs.

Then he does something wonderful. He does it every night, but it never gets boring. He gathers the corners of the washcloth into a soft, soggy bowl, fills it with warm water from the tub, and pours it down our backs to rinse us off. He usually does Fred first. I don't like watching and waiting, but it is also nice to be last. I love the trick of turning the cloth into a bowl, and I love the warmth of the bathwater on my back. Most of all, I love the attention my father is paying to me. I wait for him to do it again, and he usually does—but just once. If I ask for another turn, he says no.

After our bath, we get into bed and Dad tells us a story. This was another good thing about bedtime. Many of Dad's stories focused on two young boys, "gray-eyed George and brown-eyed Bob," who were very similar in appearance and behavior to my brown-eyed brother and me. In the great American tradition of Tom Sawyer and Huck Finn, George and Bob usually got into some kind of trouble and then got each other out of it in ways that revealed both the strengths and the limitations of their respective characters. In the only story I remember, George (that's me) fell into a well, and Bob (Fred) got him out; you will note that the younger, more active, more resourceful brother saves the older, more timid, klutzier brother.

Years later, when I bathed my own children at bedtime, I also gathered the edges of the washcloth; but my bowls were leaky and never deep enough to hold much water, and the kids probably wondered why I even attempted such an odd thing. Like Dad I told them stories that neither they nor I remember; then I tucked them into bed and prayed with them—no big deal, just "Now I lay me down to sleep," though we upgraded to the Lord's Prayer as they got older. Then, just as he did, I pulled up the covers, turned out the light, and left the room. One thing I did that he didn't: I kissed them goodnight—our sons Mark and Jamie as well as our daughter Cathy.

You may have wondered why I spent so much time describing Mercury Man's battered old car at Empire Beach. Although I am low-tech when it comes to computers, I have loved cars all my life. It was during World War II, when I was only three or four and could barely pronounce some of their names (Toodebakuh, Twyswuh), that Dad started teaching me to distinguish the different makes. We sat in front of our house where Mom didn't allow me to sit by myself, at the top of the steep steps that descended to the street. We could see a long ways in both directions. It was great for car-watching. I was a quick study and could soon distinguish the rounder lines of the new Fords, Lincoln Zephyrs, and Chryslers from the squarer silhouettes of the more expensive General Motors brands like Buick and LaSalle. I got to know Mercurys a few years later when a stolen one showed up in our driveway one day and the police came and impounded it. It was a Ford with stripes—just as a Pontiac was a striped Chevrolet.

Up to a point, Dad shared my interest in cars. You could even say it was in our blood; but for him it had been an obligation more than a passion. My grandfather owned a Chevrolet garage in Cadiz, and as a young man Dad was involved from time to time in the family business. He never trained as a mechanic, but he worked sometimes as a salesman, including the summer of 1936 before his marriage with Mom. Also, back in the thirties, new cars were not always delivered to dealers on big carrier trucks. Instead, Grandpa, Dad, his brothers, and even his older sister sometimes had to travel to Michigan to pick up new cars and drive them individually back to Cadiz to be displayed and sold. Put along with that the fact that he never had enough money to indulge any automotive fantasies—he had to confine himself to inexpensive, practical family cars—and it's easy enough to see why Dad had a more disciplined feeling for cars than I did.

One of my earliest demonstrations of car love was also one of the few times I remember being spanked by Dad. World War II was over, but my parents still saved bacon fat and other household grease to turn in for ration coupons. Fred and I were out in the garage one warm summer day looking for something important to do, something we could really put our hearts into. Leslie, our androgynously named 1936 Chevy two-door sedan—we called her "Yeswee" until our l's improved—was parked there. After the war, very few new cars were available; it took the factories a while to switch back to peacetime production. Like many other cars then, Leslie looked more than a little the worse for wear after schlepping us faithfully through the war years; her once bright green enamel had grown faded and chalky.

I'm not sure how I was inspired to make the great imaginative leap that followed; maybe it was because I had recently seen Mom wax the dining room table. I found an old rag in the garage, used it to take a dab of grease from the ration can, and smeared it onto Leslie's front fender. Immediately the chalkiness vanished, and in its place was a dazzling green shine. Granted, it was not the clear, deep gleam of a just-waxed hardwood table; it cast a slimy glitter, and it packed a piggy whiff. But I urged Fred to join me in "polishing the car." He quickly found this activity as gratifying as I did. While he took over on the fender, I started with a second rag on the spoked wheel. I worked quickly, with deep concentration, and soon had half the spokes coated with sparkly, smelly grease.

Then a large hand reached down, snatched away the rag, and slapped me on the bottom. I heard Dad's voice raised an octave higher than normal: "My God! What a terrible mess—how will I ever get it off?" I was crushed: Dad didn't like it, and besides, he immediately realized that I had gotten Fred into this. When I looked one last time at the wheel I had so lovingly greased, it no longer looked sparkly; it was nasty.

In spite of this setback, I got so good with cars that I could even tell the different makes by the sounds they made as their drivers shifted them. Medieval astronomers yearned to hear the "music of the spheres"; for me, it was the music of the gears. Today, most cars have automatic transmissions and sound about the same; but back in the forties, a Chevrolet going through the gears sounded different from a Buick. The Chevrolet made a light, cheerful sound, while the Buick's gears produced deeper, full-bodied, more substantial tones. Operatically speaking, it was the difference between a flirty soprano in a soubrette role, like Musetta in *La Bohème*, and a slinky mezzo-soprano doing *Carmen*. The Ford V-8s had a deeper, macho rumble that sounded rough, even dangerous, over the gear noises; in today's terms, they were rap artists with attitude.

When automatic shifts started to proliferate after the war, I could tell without looking if it was a Pontiac, Olds, or Cadillac with Hydra-Matic; they revved up loudly in the lower two of their four forward gears and cruised along more easily in the two higher ones. Buicks with Dynaflow emitted a unique whooshing moan, something between a large mammal in pain and a jet plane gathering thrust before takeoff. Then they slowly, slowly began moving, nearly a second after the driver had pressed the gas pedal—or so it seemed to me in my high school years when I drove to Cleveland with a friend of mine in his mother's Buick Super hardtop to visit a college he was interested in. It must have taken half a gallon of gas just to get one of those big, heavy Buicks going again after stopping it at a traffic light. Of course gas was cheap then, and nothing else on the road moaned like a Buick. At this time, most Chrysler-built cars came equipped with Fluid Drive, a semiautomatic transmission that permitted leisurely clutchless starts in third gear, but required the driver to lift his foot from the accelerator and wait for a click, indicating that the transmission had shifted into high gear, before reaching highway speeds. A few years later, while delivering newspapers on my bike, if I heard the hesitation and click behind me I didn't have to look around to know it was a practical Dodge, a toothy De Soto, or an elegant Chrysler.

The post-war Hudsons were harder to identify by sound, but it was worth turning around to see one better. They had powerful motors, good handling for that era, and what their ads proclaimed as "step-down" design: a unique, slick, adrenalin-pumping, low-slung silhouette, the automotive equivalent of some of the movie stars of those days—say Rhonda Fleming or Yvonne De Carlo. They were the first American cars to have the floor lower than the doorsill. When I watched the film version of *Driving Miss Daisy* the second time, it was as much to see her immaculate Hudson sedan as it was to see the brilliant acting by Jessica Tandy and Morgan Freeman. And when our daughter Cathy took me to the original Hudson garage in Ypsilanti one cold winter day a few years ago, I fell in love all over again. I stared and stared at one partially restored step-down sedan with two shades of dark green on its sleek, sculpted fenders. Working up my courage, as if initiating intimacy with Rhonda or Yvonne, I finally opened the driver's door and stroked the musty and rather luridly stained original upholstery. I still wish that even for just one year we could have arrived at Glen Lake in a 1950 Hudson.

When Dad was able to shop for a new car in the spring of 1948, one of the few models available for immediate purchase was a new make, a Kaiser. The Kaiser was blue, good-looking, and roomy. It also had a left rear door that often would not latch properly until just the right combination of loud slams and gentle pushes had been achieved. Dad took it back to the dealer more than once, but they never did fix it. The Kaiser was an "off-brand" and Dad knew it, but Leslie was dying of old age and he couldn't afford either the price or the wait for another Chevrolet. In any case, his clever mind came up with jokes that made us laugh hysterically and showed us all that we could have fun even if we couldn't have either a good, solid Chevy or a ritzy Cadillac like his boss and his boss's wife. It was with the Kaiser that Dad first hit on the idea of pretending to other motorists that we had an automatic shift. While my mother objected, laughing, that he would surely get us into a wreck, he would ride the clutch just enough to make the Kaiser creep forward at traffic lights the way the automatic-equipped cars did.

We actually went to Glen Lake in the Kaiser—which we named Kay, after the popular bandleader Kay Kyser—for the first couple of years until Dad's boss started loaning us the Ford Ranch Wagon, which was navy blue with big fat whitewalls. Then in 1955, on one of the happiest days of my young life, Dad brought home a stylish new Chevy sedan. It was painted a brighter green than Leslie had ever worn, either in youth or with a color-enhancing coat of bacon fat. It had a cream-colored top, a V-8 motor, and a Power Glide automatic transmission. Although air-conditioning was starting to appear in Cadillacs and other top-of-the-line brands by this time, it was still two or three cars into the future for us, and we hardly noticed or cared whether the new Chevy had it or not. Nevertheless, this lack prompted Dad's second "let's pretend" game, one we laughed about more but only played once. This was because in order to pretend our car was air-conditioned, we had to roll up all the windows on a hot day and still appear cool ourselves. We tried it, as we had done with the faux-automatic creeping, one summer Sunday on the way to church, and we must all have looked a little wilted as we walked into the sanctuary that morning.

Now it's August in Leelanau, and we have just arrived, windblown, at The Ritz. Dad gets out of the car and goes in search of Bill Salisbury, the landlord, to let him know we are here. When he appears, we remember that Bill, whom we always called Mr. Salisbury, is a small, thin man with bright, piercing eyes, a big gray moustache, and a golfer-type cap pulled down low over his sharp-featured face. He looks old to me, but wiry and tough, and I have since learned that he worked hard in various sorts of physical labor for much of his life, probably arriving in Leelanau because he had worked on railroad ferries that came across the big lake from Wisconsin. Bill was also a sportsman who umpired local baseball games and trained some local boys in boxing, a sport at which he excelled. Bill's voice was loud, but he was hard for me to understand for two reasons: one, he came from England and spoke with a heavy British accent; and two, as I learned from Dad much later, he had a cleft palate, which he hid behind his large moustache. Dad pays Bill the rest of what he owes him and asks if there are any changes to the cottage or the dock since the previous year.

One year when we arrived, my mother was furious to see that the kitchen had not been cleaned and that the oven was especially filthy. She pitched a fit, and Dad went to complain; but as they both knew only too well, it was hard to imagine that anyone other than Mom herself would clean it. Neither of the Salisburys strikes me, in memory, as the avid-cleaner type. We would not see much of Bill for the next two weeks—he deliberately kept out of the way of his renters—and we would see even less of his wife Martha, a pale, heavy woman who stayed in her house nearly all the time and only rarely might be seen walking on the path between the cottages. She was so shy and retiring that if we said hello to her, she would barely acknowledge our greetings. Dad reported once that he had overheard her singing an old song whose refrain was "Please Go Away and Let Me Sleep." What this might have inadvertently revealed about the intimate life of the Salisburys, none of us ever has had the courage to imagine.

The couple had no children and could not afford a car; when we knew them, their livelihood lay in the maintaining and renting of the cottages Bill had built over the years: The Ritz; The Salisbury, located right next to it; and The Lake View, perched precariously right on the shore of Little Glen (Bill had built up the lakeshore here just so he could build the house literally at water's edge). In addition, there was a stone house Bill had built for himself and Martha back behind The Salisbury. And near The Lake View there was what I will call The Folly, a cinderblock foundation for another lakeside house Bill never built. Instead, left open on the side towards the lake, The Folly served as the borders for a sort of faux beach or giant sandbox where we played as kids. Maybe Bill realized that if he built that house, it would block the view and impede lake access for those of us who stayed in the other cottages. Maybe he just ran out of money or energy. I don't know, but both a renovated Lake View and The Folly were still there in 2003, on the shore of Little Glen, in front of the modernized Ritz and a two-story McMansioned remake of The Salisbury.

Dad dealt fairly and kindly with the Salisburys, as he did with everyone he met, but those were not his noblest moments. So now with filial pride I begin the grand mythic narrative of my father: Sir Dad and the Horrid Bat. It fell to me to precipitate the great bat chase by waking up one unforgettable winter night in Ohio, in a confusion that quickly morphed into fear. I could see nothing at first in the darkened bedroom I shared with Fred, but I heard an eerie flapping noise. Then I saw a shadow flitting through the other shadows, and I was terrified; and yes, I realize now, with totally unforced animal-rights correctness, that the bat must have been scared too. But back then I did what any red-blooded American boy would do: I began to scream. Soon Dad came rushing into the room—and this is the point at which across time and mortality my heart goes out to him. He knew that he would have to go after the bat, but that he either would (1) not be able to catch it, (2) not know what to do with it if he did, or (3) dispatch this bat only to have others follow in quick succession, night after night, until we were all either dead from exhaustion and bat-borne diseases, or so totally mad that death would be a blessed release.

Nevertheless Dad prepared himself for battle much as Sir Gawain did when he armed himself to confront the Green Knight.

He disappeared for a few minutes while I hid under the covers and Fred, awakened by the commotion, watched the bat with sheer delight. Then Dad returned to the bedroom, only now he was Sir Dad, equipped with a warrior's heroic spear and helmet—in reality a broom to chase the bat and a floppy hat made of newspapers to keep the bat out of his hair. Taking a deep breath, he immediately started after the intruder, which was still flapping wildly around, while my muffled cries rose from beneath the blankets and Fred yelled, "Hit 'im again, Daddy, hit 'im again!" This went on until they noticed that while Sir Dad was still leaping about with the broom, the bat had disappeared.

Cautiously, I came out from under the covers. Possibly, Sir Dad said, it had returned where it came from by slipping under the closet door, which led up to the attic. All was peace and tranquility—but only for a moment. Then the dreadful flapping started again, this time from the window over Fred's bed. The bat had managed to squeeze under the window, which was opened just a crack, and had lodged itself in the space between the window and the storm window. Sir Dad ran over and closed the window so the bat could not reenter the bedroom; but neither could Sir Dad open the storm window to allow the bat to escape into the night. Exhausted and out of sorts after his heroic but inconclusive strife with the forces of darkness, he pulled down the blind and announced that the bat would have to stay trapped in the window for the rest of the night.

After turning off the light, Sir Dad left the room, taking all the chivalrous pomp of his bat-hat and broom with him, and I was left alone in the dark with Fred, who immediately fell asleep again in deep contentment. In Batman-in-Gotham fashion, the street lamp outside now projected the horrid thrashing shape of the intruder onto the drawn window shade. Though my fear remained unabated, I must eventually have fallen asleep; in the morning, miraculously, the bat had utterly disappeared from the window. And it never came back, though our memories of Sir Dad with his bat-hat and broom have remained as green as our Chevrolets.

One Saturday at home, Dad began to paint the small, square wooden porch at the back of our house. I watched him and realized that all my life I had wanted nothing more than to help paint the back porch. Not since I smeared grease onto Leslie's fender several years earlier had I felt so powerful an urge to beautify my surroundings. I begged Dad to let me paint the railing white. He said no, but I kept telling him how much I wanted to do it and how good I would be at it. Finally he gave in and let me paint. And he went inside—probably because he couldn't bear to stay and watch me make a mess.

In one of the more bizarre ironies of my clumsy young life, I painted quite neatly. The wet white paint on the brush submitted to my control as I drew it steadily across the railing. I still have what dancers call a "body memory" of how the brush felt in my hand. I was cool, calm, and powerful. I felt the same way years later, in college, when I aced the tumbling exam in my PE class by doing a perfect shoulder stand on the parallel bars while the jocks all stood agape: I wasn't supposed to be that good at it. I called into the house to tell Dad I had finished. He said to wait and he would come and take the paint and brush back into the house and down to the basement. But proud of having done so well with the railing, I decided I would help still more by bringing everything in myself.

This was a mistake. Somehow I managed to turn the paint can upside down as I entered the house. While the lid stayed stuck in place long enough for me to cross the kitchen hall and start down the basement steps, it suddenly slipped and all the paint still in the can started pouring out—down the steps, under the steps, everywhere. It leaked onto me and, horribly, even onto Dad, who was already in the basement but was about to come up and help me with the can. It seemed to us in our mutual horror to coat not only the basement and us, but the whole known world. Horror was the only emotion we shared at that moment: he didn't share my guilt, and I didn't share his fury.

It was April first, but it was still wintry-nasty in Columbus. I was probably about nine or ten—that would make it during the years of the dream-Hudsons—and somewhere I had heard about a terrific April Fool joke: you announce that canned apricots will be served for dessert, and then serve the victim a couple of raw eggs, the yolks floating in the whites. The idea was that the egg yolks would look enough like canned apricot halves to fool the person into starting to eat them. It wouldn't work today, because nobody eats canned apricots anymore, or any other kind of canned fruit. But back then, frozen fruits and vegetables were just catching on, they were expensive, the year-round availability of fresh fruits from Chile or New Zealand wasn't even imagined, and in states like Ohio and Michigan where winter meant endless nasty weather, people ate tons of canned apricots, plums, peaches, and cherries. I thought this apricot trick was the funniest thing I had ever heard of—partly, no doubt, because of the deeply conflicted feelings about eggs to which I have already confessed—so I asked Mom to serve Dad this horrible dessert that night after dinner. She didn't want to do it. And who could blame her for wanting to spare both the eggs and my father this assault? But I kept begging her to do it, so finally she agreed.

Dad would have to have had apricots—or eggs—for brains not to know that something was going on that evening. I was so excited that I must have gotten up and run into the kitchen three times while Mom cleared the plates. Finally she brought out the vile cholesterol-laced faux fruit. It was a disaster: even I could see that the eggs looked like eggs and that no one could possibly confuse them with apricot halves. Worse, Dad didn't think it was funny, I could tell, though he pretended halfheartedly that he enjoyed the trick. I felt depressed and sad—not so much that the trick had failed, but that it had failed to amuse him. I see now that unlike most of the humor at our house, this joke was not verbal but visual, not subtle but crude—a sight gag—and we didn't ordinarily go in for practical joking of this sort. Since neither Dad nor I were athletic, he couldn't teach me how to throw or bat a ball. I had to rely on my ability to please him with my wit—and this didn't, and Mom knew it wouldn't.

In an ironic reversal of the botched April Fool's joke, it was one of Dad's quiet kindnesses to me that ended up making me the butt of a joke at our dinner table. I have worn glasses since I was three, so as a child I had to have my vision checked regularly. Even in the primitive forties, the eye doctor used drops to dilate my eyes for the examination. The difference is that back then, one's pupils stayed dilated for hours and hours afterward, making vision blurry and bright lights painful right up to bedtime. After my checkup one year, I had trouble seeing at dinner, not to mention that I felt cross and sorry for myself. That night, Mom cooked Swiss steak that had a lot of fat on the edges. I hated the soft, slippery bites of fat that got into my mouth; like eggs, they made me gag. I tried to trim my meat myself with my knife and fork, but since my eyes were still dilated, I couldn't see well enough to do it.

Dad saw that I was having trouble, so he volunteered to trim it for me. I passed my plate over to him, he quickly cut off the fat, and then he handed the plate back. I started eating and immediately thought there was fat, not meat, in my mouth—but Dad had been so nice that I didn't want to say anything. I must have worn a tragic expression, however, because everyone else looked at my plate and me—and then laughed. Still partially blinded by the eye drops, I had begun eating the pile of fat Dad trimmed away instead of the good bites of beef. I still remember this as a terrible moment when once again I feel I had failed my father. At least— are you ready for this?—I proved there was more than one way to "chew the fat" at a family dinner.

Dad loved crossword puzzles. He always did the small one in the daily newspaper and the bigger one in the Sunday paper. He even did them at Little Glen. A new book of crossword puzzles was always a good Christmas or birthday present for Dad. Gradually, over time, he got Fred, Molly, and me interested in doing them, and he taught us his crossword solution process. First, he told us, we should go through all the clues and write in immediately all the answers we were completely sure of. These include, but of course are not limited to, names of state and national capitals, mountain ranges and rivers, movie titles, movie stars, athletes, politicians, and famous book titles. Once we had a sure word in place, then we were to look at all the immediately surrounding word clues in order to enter more words.

He also told us with stern irony that there are "crossword puzzle words" we had to learn if we wanted to be any good at solving them. These are words which, while theoretically found in dictionaries and used in writing and conversation, in fact appear only in crossword puzzles. Among these are certain animals (llama, gnu, emu, okapi, moray, eland, erne); a handful of place names (Sault Sainte Marie, Michigan, usually reduced to its nickname "Soo," or its canonized middle section "Ste.," is a prime example; so is Agra, the city in India where the Taj Mahal is located); and a few titles or honorifics ("rani," the wife of a Hindu rajah, seems indispensable to crossword-puzzle designers, but "rajah" too gets a lot of play, as do "emir" and "Srta.," the Spanish abbreviation for "Señorita"). I have similarly coached our children, who all spend good time doing crosswords that they could use to do other things that would advance humanity more.

If Dad hadn't been working hard in his office one warm, un-air-conditioned afternoon, we would never have known our dog Mickey. It's a classic story: the knightly, gracious hero, Sir Dad but without the bat-hat, saves the cute abandoned puppy that whimpers for attention in a busy, dangerous place. Dad thought he heard a noise from outside whenever he stopped typing, so he looked out the opened window, saw nothing, typed some more, looked out again, and there was Mickey, sitting on the narrow strip of grass between the side of Dad's one-floor office building and the parking lot of the White Castle hamburger restaurant next door. How did the little guy get separated from his mother? How did he make it across the parking lot without getting hit by a car? Perhaps someone abandoned him there in the grass on purpose. We never knew. Mickey's appearance suggested that one parent was a boxer, but offered no clues as to the other. He had a boxer's short brown and white hair and legs, but the shape of his head was more like that of the RCA Victor "His Master's Voice" dog, with floppy ears. He had a white underbelly, a white tip to his tail, and—his most striking feature—one black eye. This made us think of the children in the *Our Gang* comedies, and that is how he got named Mickey McGuire McGavran.

He came along at a good time for our family. We had briefly had another dog that we had to return to the animal shelter because she had bitten a girl in the neighborhood—or so the girl's mother said. We didn't like the girl and thought Brownie had shown good sense to bite her. We missed Brownie. Besides, we were just old enough to enjoy having a dog around and to take some responsibility for feeding, walks, and baths. Mickey won our hearts that day, immediately becoming the sixth member of the family. He was exuberantly friendly and totally harmless, to us and to other people as well—once he was housebroken, a task that fell to Mom.

I used to take Mickey for long walks in Miller Park, near our house; I loved being out alone with the dog and running with him. In fact, I would have taken him to my secret beach on Little Glen, but he wouldn't get into the rowboat. At the far end of the park was a culvert that formed a passageway under a busy street; to there Mickey and I would trek, and from there we would start our return back though the park to our house. I don't know how he felt about it, but I loved to linger there, listening to the cars pass on the road above us, and trying to identify them by their whines, moans, rumbles, and clicks.

From the time Dad found him, Mickey always accompanied us on our annual trips to Leelanau. We did the things travelers usually do for their pets: we leashed him and walked him when we stopped at roadside parks, carried some dog food and water, and generally reassured him that he was OK on the trip. This last did not take much doing, since he always loved getting into the car and taking off. Once we were installed at The Ritz, Mickey usually accompanied us to Little Glen when we swam, to the sand dunes, and to the Empire Beach picnics. He was wary of jumping into the big lake, but Little Glen held no terrors for him—only for us, since as soon as he came out he would shake himself off, and whoever was closest to him would receive a doggy-scented shower of lake water. The worst thing that ever happened to Mickey in Leelanau was the time he chased a porcupine in the woods and received a noseful of quills for his trouble. Mom labored for at least an hour over his poor tender nose, using a disinfectant and pulling out the barbed quills as gently as possible.

Dad brought Mickey into our lives, and fourteen years later it was Dad who took him, aged and failing, to the vet's to be euthanized. He always was especially close to Dad, perhaps associating him with his first entry into our family. Dad did not always welcome this intimacy, especially in Mickey's later years when he would always lie down by Dad's chair after dinner, farting frequently and copiously all evening while Dad tried to read. Dad's clever solution to this problem was to keep a book of matches by his chair so that as soon as Mickey passed some gas, Dad could ignite it. This fact regarding the behavior of combustible gases—or is it the combustion of behavioral gases?—might not excite a scientist, but to an English major like me, it seemed a miracle that igniting the fart actually made the odor go away. No chemistry major himself, Dad once explained the source of his uncanny knowledge: at a fraternity party at Ohio State in his college days, he had seen a match lit and flaring at the bare behind of one of the brothers.

I liked to look at my report cards from school because usually they were all A's except for PE; I was a smart little geek. I would always turn the card over and see that my father had signed it for each six-weeks grading period. I studied his signatures and marveled how each one seemed exactly the same as the others—firm and bold, except once where he used a different pen, so that one was lighter, paler, blue instead of black. "James H. McGavran": his name, and mine too, since I am a junior. Could I write my name five times in a row and make each one look like all the others? I went up to my room with a sheet of paper and started practicing. Not only did my signatures not look neatly alike; they all looked weak and wobbly. Would I ever be able to sign my name with such authority? It awed me, but it also made me proud to see my father's signature on my card. This made my grades official. He had acknowledged my academic accomplishments.

A little later, in my language arts class I learned how to answer the telephone—and it turned out that "Hello" was wrong. Instead, according to the textbook, one should say "Harrisons' residence, Jack speaking." Since I had never in my life heard anyone say anything but "Hello" when picking up a phone, I was first fascinated and then worried: had my parents' telephone manners been faulty all these years?

It must have been a Saturday, because it was daytime, Dad was home, and Mom was not around. No doubt she had taken advantage of Dad's presence to go out shopping. Fred, Molly, and I were sitting with Dad around the breakfast table. While he worked at the crossword puzzle in the paper, I was studying my textbook. I decided to read him this information on telephone etiquette, at once disapproving of our own family practice and teetering on the brink of absurdity—and thus ripe for subversion. Dad was intrigued and immediately got us to disputing whether the textbook should be taken literally or whether we should insert our own names. Then, just as abruptly answering his own question, he declared that the authors intended not a substitution here but rather that everyone, everywhere, should use these same four words.

We were all laughing by then at the idiocy of the textbook writers when the phone rang. Dad picked it up, and as if to teach us a good lesson, he actually said, "Harrisons' residence, Jack speaking." There was an explosion of caller anger at the other end of the line, loud enough to be audible across the table. Dad's face became a study in contrasting emotions: he seemed mortified, but he was also struggling to keep from laughter. He continued to listen, said a few words more into the mouthpiece, and then hung up. Now laughing out loud, he told us that it was his boss who had called. This was very unusual. Mr. King never bothered Dad at home about work, so it may have had to do with a social event, perhaps an "office party" to be held at the Kings' elegant home. He was a hard-boiled, impatient, successful alpha male and not the type to "suffer fools gladly." While he would never have thought of Dad as a fool—Dad's writing was what held the magazine together—Dad knew from experience when it was OK to joke with him. Since Mr. King was preoccupied with delivering his message that Saturday morning, it was not one of those times. His response, edited by Dad I'm sure, ran along the lines of "Jim? What the hell, Jim, is that you? For God's sake, why don't you say 'Hello' when you answer the phone, like everyone else?"

As a teenager I was not very happy—the class brain, geeky, shy, unathletic. But introverted as I was, I still used to like going out in the car with Dad when he did his Saturday morning errands. There was probably a school project I should have been working on, which was part of why getting out of the house could suddenly become so attractive. But that wasn't the whole reason. As diffident as he could be in large groups, Dad showed another side of his personality now: his Saturday rounds made me admire his easy way of interacting with the people around him. While my parents enjoyed cocktails at parties and manhattans at Empire Beach, their everyday imbibing was strictly low-budget: Gambrinus, an inexpensive local beer, in the summer, and Roma sherry in the wintertime. We entered the local beer-and-wine store, and Dad conversed easily, familiarly, with the old man who clerked there. It was nothing deep—it could have been the weather, or something he had heard on the radio—but enough to make the routine purchase take on the feel of an elaborate social ritual. How did he do it? I was watching, listening, but I had no idea. Years later, I found I could do it myself; all it took was to start talking, trying to see things from other people's perspectives, but without patronizing them. Maybe if I'd discovered this sooner, I'd have become a politician—or a preacher. But Dad's remembered social graces still help me as a teacher to communicate more effectively with my university students.

After carrying the Gam or the Roma out to the car, we would go next door to the drycleaner's. The woman who worked there was named Mary, and she carried a torch for my father. She had longish gray hair pulled back from her face, but she was not as old as her hair first made her appear; in fact she was quite pretty, and her eyes sparkled as soon as she saw Dad walk into the shop. Smoking by this time had robbed my father of some of his youthful good looks; his skin was starting to lose its color. But most other men smoked in those times, Dad was remarkably trim for a man in a sedentary job, there was a bounce in his step, and he often caught women's appraising eyes.

The best proof that Dad was not having an affair with Mary is that he had already told Mom about her. In fact, as we left the house on those Saturday mornings, Mom would tell me jokingly to say hello to Mary for her. The thing that is hard to describe is, again, how effortlessly charming Dad was. No wonder Mary had developed a thing about him. Without flirting, he spoke to her at a level of friendliness far above what most people would show to a shop clerk, and she responded gratefully as she gathered his washed and pressed office shirts, turning her smile to me and saying something trite but kind about what a fine young man I was, or how bad the weather was. Later, back at home, Mom would ask teasingly for a report on our meeting with Mary.

Though sternly moralistic on many issues, Dad liked to see movie versions of the kind of plays my mother called sordid or trashy. As I got older, he seemed to like to hear me talk about films like Tennessee Williams's *Cat on a Hot Tin Roof*, with Paul Newman and Elizabeth Taylor, or, later, Edward Albee's *Who's Afraid of Virginia Woolf?* starring Taylor with Richard Burton. Mom wouldn't go to see movies like these, but once, when I was on a visit home from graduate school, I noticed in the newspaper that the RKO Palace, one of the big old downtown movie theaters, advertised a second-run showing of *Who's Afraid*. I had already seen it, but I wanted to see it again. Feeling suddenly inspired, I asked Dad if he would like to go and see it with me—and he agreed. Over dinner, my mother felt compelled to go on quite a bit about decadence, and she did, but then Dad and I left for the theater.

It was the late 1960s, and already the old Columbus downtown was starting to die; shortly the Palace and its across-the-street rival Loew's Broad would be permanently closing their doors. There were few cars on the street, and even fewer people in the theater, as I recall, when we entered. After we watched the film, we said little to each other on the way home. But I could tell that Dad had been excited and moved by Albee's relentless exposure of the small and large tensions of marriage. I couldn't usually recommend new books that I read to Dad, because he always thought that anything I liked would be too intellectual, too pretentious for him. He tended to prefer popular novelists like James Michener, and mystery writers like Erle Stanley Gardner. But I felt close to him, as if we had made a significant cultural connection, as we drove home from *Who's Afraid of Virginia Woolf?*

Five months before my father died, he called from Columbus and told me he wanted to buy me a new suit for Christmas: "Take yourself shopping, get something nice, and send me the bill." At first I protested what seemed a generous but poorly timed offer, immediately thinking of several other things that would be more useful for the kids or the house. I told him I already had a perfectly good charcoal gray wool suit with pinstripes—it couldn't have been more than five years old. Although I didn't tell him so, it wasn't worn out because I hardly ever put it on, preferring instead the tweeds, corduroys, and khakis that make up my academic wardrobe. But he insisted, so late in November 1993, I bought the suit—fine black wool this time, not gray, and with wider spaces between the pinstripes. In January, just before his eighty-fourth birthday, Dad learned that he had cancer: a tumor on his left lung was metastasizing, surgery was not worth the risks, and palliative care and Hospice were the best that could be done. He was dead in six weeks. I wore the new suit to his funeral.

I have always associated the suit with his final illness and death, but I never found out whether he did. Dad had paid attention to my clothes—my dress-up clothes, that is—ever since I was in seventh grade and he took me downtown to Morehouse-Martens on a gray Ohio winter day to buy my very first "grownup" suit. That was when he started to teach me where to look to judge the fit of a suit or sport jacket: not just the correct cuff and trouser length, but details like the degree of tapering on the sides of the jacket and the lay of the collar on the shoulders. Years later, when Deje and I came back to Columbus with the kids for a visit, he would encourage me to look at the end-of-season sale at his favorite men's shop and reimburse me if I bought something.

But by this time in our lives, decades had passed since major clothing purchases had been standard gift items from him and my mother. He had spoken to Mom all that autumn, I found out later, of an unusual fatigue, a heaviness that he couldn't shake off. Perhaps he suspected even before the diagnosis that he was mortally ill. Did he buy the suit as a final gift for his firstborn and namesake? Or was he afraid that I would disgrace the family by shambling into his digni-fied Presbyterian funeral looking like Mr. Chips meets the Dead Poets' Society? In spite of all those easygoing summer days in Leelanau, my parents had come to set great store by appearances at this time in their lives. The retirement center where they chose to spend their last years required residents to dress for dinner every night—jackets and ties for the men and skirts for the women—and they loved this formality. Now Dad gave specific instructions about his funeral: who would read from the Bible (my brother-in-law John, not me, since he knew I would just get up and cry) and which pas-sages. He also chose the hymns that were to be sung: "Our God Our Help in Ages Past" and the "Battle Hymn of the Republic."

I wore these suspicions along with the black suit to the funeral, and to the bitter cold burial on a windy hilltop in Cadiz, where he would lie near his parents and grandparents and two of his siblings who had preceded him in death. On the drive back to Columbus, I tried to separate Mom from her grief by comment-ing on the wintry beauty decking the forlorn, familiar eastern Ohio hills. She had always responded with passion to nature—in the state parks of Ohio as in the forests of Leelanau—but now she remained inconsolable in a way that was prophetic of her subse-quent decline into depression and dementia. I should have realized it, though, because in his final weeks, Dad repeatedly told us he was worried about how Mom would get along without him. What he knew, but had previously hidden from us on our visits, was that she was already beginning to lose her memory.

Suddenly the clouds shifted, and brilliant sunlight glittered through the ice on the trees and over the snow covering the ground. It was an eclipse in reverse, an eclipse of light. Blinded on the curving highway, I flipped down the visor and reached awkwardly for my sunglasses. Squinting, still dazzled, I was also immensely gladdened. Here in the midst of death and winter's cold, sky and earth were ablaze—not mocking our grief, but reminding me of the delight Dad had brought to so many other people for so long—his family, his friends, the singers at Empire Beach, and even Mary at the cleaner's and the man in the wine store, who were cheered just to see him walk into their shops. Was my father up there some-where behind the sunlight? Was he laughing—or annoyed—at my suspicions about the new suit? I can't say, but I know I felt closer to him then than at any time since his death.

As I continued to drive Mom back to Columbus, I recalled, as I often still do, the last time I saw my father alive. I had taken him to meet with his oncologist; I heard the prognosis along with him. And I heard his amazing response. Grateful to know the truth, he thanked the doctor with a simple grace, an elegance of spirit that danced straight through my ears into my memory. I thought I already knew how much I loved him; but in that moment, when Dad's biological clock was running down, love grew beyond all bounds—along with the realization that once again, as with so many of the things I had learned from him over the years, I had just been handed an impec-cable script for my own last act, should I get the chance to play it. As we left the doctor's office, I felt so close to him, so full of the life he had shared with me for so long, that I almost didn't tell him how much I admired his strength and calm; it seemed superfluous some-how. But I did tell him, and that turned out to be a crucial decision, since I was not to get a second chance.

Equally crucial, but far less fortunate, was the decision I made regarding another of Dad's comments during that last visit home. We were out in the car together and talking about nothing in par-ticular when he said, out of the blue, "Well, I've done some pretty bad things in my life." What "pretty bad things" could my dear, dying father have done? I was speechless with surprise just at the moment when I should have responded, "Is there something you want to tell me?" It certainly sounded like the prelude to a confession, but I thought I could circle back to it later. Not realizing how little time he had left, Deje and I left for North Carolina the next day. He died sooner than we expected, before we could get up to see him again—and I will never know what it was he was thinking of telling me. Now, in the car with my mother, I silently thanked him for all he had given of himself for so long: his wit and energy, his artistry with words and music, his modeling of a kind of manhood that did not require athletic prowess or other purely physical might, but rested instead on intelligence, charm, and kindness.

Shortly after the burial, Mom decided that she wanted to give Dad's clothes to their church for distribution to people in need. While sorting through them, I found a brown tweed sport jacket that Dad had kept for so long that it had been downgraded from "good" to "everyday." Although it was no longer spiffy enough for dress occasions, I remembered he had even worn it to do his Saturday errands. I took it and taught in it for about four years, until it had almost fallen apart. I stopped wearing it, but I kept it. Then I bought a replacement as similar to Dad's old one as possible; it is still intact, but has already had to have part of its lining resewn. A decade after Dad's death, the black wool was the only suit I owned. I never planned to buy another one—until Cathy's wedding, when I finally did.

Missing Dad all over again as I write, suddenly in my mind I am once more in Leelanau, a child in the back seat with my brother and sister and Mickey. It's hot at The Ritz this afternoon, so we are going to Glen Haven to cool off in the big lake. As we drive up

M-109, I look out the left window at the Sleeping Bear parking lot. At the refreshment stand there, they sell Squirt, a grapefruit-flavored soda that I like. Thinking about Squirt, I ask if we can climb the sand dune before we go to Glen Haven. Mom says it's too hot to climb the sand dunes and tells me to look out the other side of the car and see the Day farmhouse. I look and see the house, and the barn too. Compared to Squirt, they are big and white and boring.

Then through the windshield I see the big lake, all blue-green and sparkly with North Manitou right in front of us. Dad drives down the big hill to the beach and parks. Now both Manitous are off to the left and very close-looking. Mom reminds us about the old dock. Gulls like to sit on the posts that stick up out of the water, but other posts are hidden under the waves and we have to watch out for them as we swim. When we wade out into the cold lake, stones on the bottom hurt my feet. Then we're beyond the stones—jumping, surface-diving, and paddling around. Mom and Molly are keeping a little off to themselves. Mickey has stayed on the beach; the big lake makes him nervous.

Fred and I are swimming with Dad. Dad always swims with his head out of the water, turning from side to side with each stroke to breathe. It isn't a good way to swim, but it's the only way he can do it. He calls it his Cadiz stroke, because hardly anyone in Cadiz knew how to swim and there was no one who could teach him the crawl. Fred splashes at Dad to get his attention, but I'm afraid to do anything that might annoy him. Instead, treading water like mad, I call to him: "Daddy, Daddy!" I squeal, "Daddy!" I'm not sure whether what comes next is memory or fantasy—I so much want to believe it happened. My father swims straight at me, smiling, tanned from the Leelanau sun, and reaches out to take me in his arms.

PART FOUR

CONCERTS, CROSSINGS, KINSHIP, LOVE

It was a clear July evening in 2001, just two days after I cornered my parents' ghosts in The Ritz, when Deje and I drove to the Sleeping Bear dune climb for a special event. Since 1998, the Glen Arbor Art Association has sponsored an annual summer concert at the dunes; on this night, members of the Traverse Symphony Orchestra would perform. We were ten minutes early, but the main parking lot was already full. Shuttle buses were bringing people to the dunes from a remote lot on Little Glen, but we only found that out later—so like many others, we parked along M-109 and walked in. All around us, people were carrying chairs, blankets, and big coolers. The closer we got to the listening area in front of the climbing face, the more I sensed the excitement in the air.

The concert was late getting started; the musicians had apparently decided, given the size of the crowd, to allow people more time to arrive and get settled. Recorded music was played, and we relaxed into our short-legged beach chairs and began people-watching. The demographic was mixed: from some packs and coolers appeared hors d'oeuvres accompanied by frosty chardonnay, while from others emerged Doritos, sandwiches, and ice cream bars to be washed down with Cokes or beer. All around us, children darted quick as crickets between groups of seated adults, some running partway up the dune while parents called them back in that flat, "I-can't-believe-you're-doing-this-to-me-now" tone that indicated they were not about to enforce the command. Other people waved frantically, calling out over the noise of the crowd to attract the attention of friends just arriving.

I think of Mom and Dad whenever I find myself at the Sleeping Bear end of Little Glen; this is "our" Leelanau, within a few hundred yards of The Ritz, "our" cottage. So as we waited for the concert to begin, I began to ponder their decidedly varied musical tastes. More than Dad, my mother enjoyed classical as well as popular music, especially the spectacle and passion of grand opera. All of a sudden I was back home in Columbus, housebound in one of the endless gray, dreary winters of my childhood. It was Saturday afternoon, and Mom was listening to the Texaco Metropolitan Opera radio broadcast. She had turned the volume up high on the radio-phonograph in the living room so she could hear it in the kitchen while she cooked. Emcee-commentator Milton Cross always read the cast lists and summarized the plot of each act. Phrases like "swear eternal enmity," "yearns for her lover's return," and "falls lifeless to the floor" flowed from his patrician lips every week; there was both horror and fascination in his tone, as if he had just discovered that there was a wrong side of the tracks. During the intermissions, other voices unlike any I had heard in Columbus—voices perhaps native to Milan, or Marseilles, or Munich—answered, often at great length, the questions posed on "Opera Quiz."

Dutiful about art, as with so many other things in her life, Mom knew it was "good music" and she should appreciate it and try to pass it on to her children. But the plain truth is that she loved it. She would snap her fingers like make-believe castanets when Bizet's Carmen strutted her stuff in front of Don José. While weaving a delicate lattice crust over a cherry pie, she might hum along with Verdi's soaring, heartbreaking melody as the desperate African princess Aida, enslaved by her haughty Egyptian love-rival Amneris, begged the gods first for pity and then for death: "Numi pietà . . . fammi morir." Or her tears would fall into the pot of the chicken she was boiling while Puccini's Floria Tosca sang her magnificent aria "Vissi d'arte, vissi d'amore": "I have lived for art, for love."

Yes, I know it now as she did then—and like her, easily moved to tears, I can never sit through an opera performance, or even listen to a recording, dry-eyed. But as a child I found it too strange, far-off, and foreign to wrap my Midwestern brain around. Mom did what any good teacher would do: she reviewed the plot; she hummed the major melodies and themes and told me to listen for them; but most of all, she wanted me to feel the characters' overwhelming emotions as she did. Still it often sounded more like screaming than singing, and I wished the weather was good enough for me to escape and play outdoors.

One dreadful Saturday, driven by screeching soprano or caterwauling tenor—I don't recall which, and it hardly matters—I remember going out, over the objections of everyone else, even my brother Fred, who ordinarily would have thought it a great idea to go outside and play in a sleet storm. But I was no sooner out the door and past the porch railing than I slipped and fell on my tailbone on the ice that coated our back sidewalk—the same sidewalk where the previous spring I had garroted myself on the clothesline when I couldn't figure out how to stop my new two-wheeler bike except with my neck. Thus brought low on the site of my earlier debacle, I shuffled tearfully back inside a minute later, condemned to hear not just the opera but a family chorus of "I told you so." At least there might be creamed chicken or cherry pie to look forward to at dinnertime.

Years later, when against all likelihood I showed interest in opera, Mom sent me to the basement for some heavy maroon albums that had belonged to her parents, Fred and Dellmer Jaeger. I found a treasure. Here was the great Enrico Caruso singing the *verismo* arias that made him an international superstar before that term was even in use: roles like Turiddu in *Cavalleria Rusticana* and Canio in *Pagliacci*. Here I also met Geraldine Farrar, the great American singing actress of the World War I era, who often costarred with Caruso at the Met. The old 78 rpms were already scratched and sprung in their centers when I started listening to them, so they wobbled and surged and ticked while the recording limitations of that time gave the voices a tinny, faraway quality. But even then I showed the technophobic tendencies that make me shy away today from new computer applications (Have I yet confessed to you that I am challenged even to double-click at the proper speed?), and I actually valued those old records all the more for their auditory imperfections. For me, they provided a reminder both eerie and strangely soothing that Caruso, Farrar, and their contemporaries were part of the past, that these were the voices of the dead.

Radio music on those winter Saturdays did not cease with the curtain calls and cheering audiences of the Met broadcasts. We were more eclectic than that. In the evening after dinner, my father would tune in "The Midwestern Hayride," a country-and-western program that came from WLW in Cincinnati. I'm not quite sure why Dad liked the "Hayride." In that age of what now seems radiant bigotry, we tended to look down on anyone we knew who came from, or was even suspected of coming from, immediately to the south of us. West Virginia and Kentucky citizens, I hate to say it, but this means you. And the music Dad played usually lay more in the mainstream pop tradition—though he occasionally drifted towards Dixie with songs like the "Tennessee Waltz" or "Stars Fell on Alabama."

It was quite a segue from Risë Stevens's sultry Carmen, Zinka Milanov's impassioned Aida, or Renata Tebaldi's elegant Tosca to hear a down-home woman named Bonnie Lou perform her signature classic, "He Taught Me How to Yodel, a-yo-de-lay-de-lay-HEE-hoo," or the Turner brothers, Zeb and Zeke, croon an Appalachian necrology called "Hillbilly Heaven," in which all the singers who had ever performed on the "Hayride" were imagined to have passed and become twinkling individual points in a "star-spangled night." Did I despise this music or look down on my father because of it? Not at all—I loved it. For me, Bonnie Lou's star shone every bit as bright as Risë's, Zinka's or Renata's, and she clearly had a better shot at eternal life than any of those bad opera ladies whose carryings-on so shocked and titillated Milton Cross. Even today I would hate to have to choose between the Countess's ravishing aria from Mozart's *Marriage of Figaro*, "Dove sono i bei momenti?" ("Where have the beautiful moments gone?") and Tammy Wynette's passive-aggressive country anthem, "If You're Born a Woman, You're Born to Be Hurt." They're singing about the same thing anyway.

However they may have diverged on Saturdays, my parents' musical tastes found common ground in the popular music they had both grown up with, and which Dad played so well. Mom used to reminisce fondly about Paul Whiteman's orchestra and Rudy Vallee, the heartthrob male singer of her youth. She also liked to recall dancing at Valley Dale, a barn-like nightclub in

East Columbus, where nationally known bands like Whiteman's performed back in the twenties. She loved the huge, many-faceted glass ball that hung from the center of the ceiling and threw darts of colored light all about the darkened dance floor. The ball was still turning and glittering when I went there on a couple of dates in the early sixties.

From Dad I heard worshipful stories of the torch singer Helen Morgan, who used to sit on top of the piano in Manhattan nightclubs to perform her signature songs from Oscar Hammerstein and Jerome Kern's *Showboat*: "Can't Help Lovin' That Man" and "Bill." Later, when I was living in New York and working on my master's degree at Columbia, I found a Morgan reissue album and gave it to Dad; it inspired him to start playing some of her songs again. I learned to play them too, songs like "Don't Ever Leave Me," and "What'll I Do?" which instantly replays in my mind now whenever I think of Dad and Mom: "What'll I do when you are far away, and I am blue, what'll I do?"

These mixed musical tastes influenced me, of course. I studied classical piano through high school, sang in school and church choirs, but also learned from Dad to play pop music by ear. They must have had some effect on our children, too. In her dancing days at Kenyon College, Cathy moved to everything from Vivaldi to Enya to Gilbert and Sullivan. Mark has become a skilled guitarist who likes to play old Beatles songs and has also discovered the work of Django Reinhardt, the French gypsy jazz guitarist of the 1930s. And Jamie excels in classical piano, with a preference for composers like Scriabin and Rachmaninoff who complement his graduate studies in Russian literature.

Finally the Traverse Symphony musicians appeared onstage and I returned from my reverie to the present. We thought we knew what to expect, but still the moment was astonishing when it arrived, so gorgeous yet incongruous it was to hear the lush, elegiac harmonies of Edvard Grieg's "From Holberg's Time: Suite for String Orchestra" as they filled our ears and then rose beyond us up the sand, faster than the children could run, before dispersing into the night. Or perhaps not incongruous: in the shelter of the great dune, so majestic and yet so vulnerable to the elements and to tourists' climbing feet, the structure and power of the music combined with the evanescence of live performance to form an exact double parallel.

Dad would have enjoyed the evening for the people-watching—as I have—and for the fact that the orchestra members were following the lead of his accordion concerts at Empire Beach half a century ago. But with her taste for the "finer things in life," my mother might have found something more in it; she would have appreciated it as a cultural event and loved the cool, weird elegance of it. And she would have dragged us to hear it whether we wanted to or not. Ghost-pondering again, I wondered whether she and Dad were there with us.

As we left the concert, I realized for the first time that someday I would have to perform my own dune music: I would have to bring Dad's old accordion back to Leelanau and take it down to the beach. But we have returned to Leelanau every year since then, with the accordion, and for the first three of those years I couldn't do it. It was sheer cowardice, I told myself, but it wasn't simple stage fright; I'd played it often for friends at home, and once in the pit orchestra for a musical play on my campus. Nor was I afraid of crying in public, or that someone else on the beach that night would call out drunkenly to stop the goddamn noise. No, it was stranger than that. It's the fear I felt when I first approached The Ritz after forty years of absence—the fear of who or what might come when I called, the fear I would actually raise ghosts. But still I knew I would do it sometime. In my mind Deje and I will drive to Empire with a picnic and a thermos full of ice-cold manhattans. We will drink and eat at one of those splintery old tables perched unevenly on the dune. There they are in the pine trees, the old tables, the ones I've seen for years only in the tiny black-and-white snapshots. Fred and Molly will be standing by, but they will be small children again, crowned with the faded, torn baseball caps we all wore back then. Our kids will be there too, but under their caps I'll hardly be able to tell them from my siblings. I know the song I have to play first:

> With someone like you, a pal good and true,
> I'd like to leave it all behind, and go and find
> Someplace that's known to God alone,
> Just a spot to call our own . . .

I'll pick up the instrument and slide on the shoulder straps. I'll stretch my left hand into the chord strap and my right over the keyboard, and I'll feel Dad's ancient squeeze-box embrace me back as I wrap it into my arms. I'll turn towards the lake, towards the setting sun. I'll be crying by now, but I won't stop, no, I'll play it straight through to the end: "We'll find perfect peace, where joys never cease . . ." Then there *will* be peace—and that's when I'll hear that other dune music, the haunted music of Leelanau: the waves lapping at the shore, the wind blowing across the big lake from past the islands, all the way from Wisconsin—no, further, from Canada and beyond, way, way out in the dark . . .

Of course it didn't happen that way. I finally did play the accordion on the beach, and "With Someone Like You" was the first song. But it was at Good Harbor Bay, not at Empire, and I didn't play it at the wedding of Catherine and Andrew, where it would have been far too intrusive, but the next evening, after they had left for their honeymoon in Alaska. To my relief, it connected me not with ghosts but with the living—family members and friends who were able to stay an extra day after the wedding, but also strangers with whom we shared the beach that night and who left their campfires to walk over and say things like "Good Idea!" "Great, Man!" or "Mellow Sounds!" All my fears and hang-ups about playing the squeeze-box had vanished because the wedding the day before had brought such a complete union of past and present, dead and living, that I had nothing left to worry about. But I need to back up a bit, to tell you more about Leelanau and more about my strange, wacky, but high-achieving McGavran family.

Two days after Molly and I searched for heart-rocks at Empire Beach in 2004, Fred arrived in Leelanau. The next morning all three of us stood on the upper deck of Mishi-Mokwa, the ferry named for the Sleeping Bear that would soon leave Leland's Fishtown Harbor for its daily run over to South Manitou Island. Deje waved from the small park near the docks; a minor but painful leg injury kept her from joining us. The ferry's motor had been throbbing, impatiently it seemed, for several minutes. The trip would begin at 10 a.m. and end at 6 p.m., when the boat returned to Leland. Allowing for the hour-and-a-half crossing time each way, we day-trippers would have just five hours on the island.

Fred and I had taken the boat trip the previous summer, but we took too many side paths and ran out of time before we could walk all the way across to the sand dunes on the west side of the island. This time Molly would lead her sluggard brothers, and we were all determined to make it to the dunes and back again. I had a more private hope as well, driven by the confused feelings I experienced whenever I looked out towards the Manitous from

Sleeping Bear: when I could look from the island dunes back towards the mainland, the burden of longing for my parents would somehow be shifted, perhaps even lightened.

The sky was clouding up, the air grew heavy with moisture; it was a far less promising day for the trip than the one Fred and I had chosen the year before, when bright sun and a brisk breeze made for a glorious outing. I began to worry that bad weather would keep us from reaching our goal today. Sure enough, we had a few sprinkles as we passed the Whaleback, the promontory that separates Leland from the north end of Good Harbor Bay. But then the rain let up, and we settled down on the upper deck for the rest of the crossing. With Fred and Molly flanking me, I started thinking about Dad and his family, and their unique combination of high spirits and high jinks with stern Protestant morality and worldly ambition.

The McGavrans of Cadiz, Ohio, were as strange a combination of dreamers and doers, the offbeat and the strait-laced, as any middle-class family I have read about in literature. This includes the Thurbers of Columbus, as James Thurber recorded them in *My Life and Hard Times*, and the fictional Bennets of Longbourn found in Jane Austen's *Pride and Prejudice*. Dad's grandfather was the town doctor for many years, a pillar of the community if ever there was one. His oldest son Charles, whom we knew as "Uncle Doctor," also became a respected physician, moving to Columbus to practice; the youngest, George, went to Detroit and succeeded in business there. My grandfather Frank stayed in Cadiz and ran a Chevrolet dealership; he later was elected Harrison County auditor. He probably felt less successful than his well-to-do brothers, but with my grandmother Mary Virginia Holt he created the biggest family—five children and eleven grandchildren. And they created something else too: the atmosphere of self-deprecating but saving humor that always prevailed when two or more McGavrans were gathered together. Whenever we saw our cousins—for Thanksgiving, Christmas, a spring picnic at a state park, or even a funeral—we laughed ourselves silly at all the crazy things that happened to McGavrans. Or that didn't happen: our stories featured weak nerves and failures as often as successes. According to the family Bible, there was even a McGavran who emigrated to America and then, apparently panicking, returned to Ireland.

Behind both the conviviality and the wry hopelessness lay Grandpa's devotion to storytelling. For him, life made sense if you could make a story out of it. He loved hearing stories and he loved telling them—qualities that must have served him well in the Chevrolet business and probably helped to draw him into politics as well. When Fred, Molly, and I were young, he told us tall tales of his youthful prowess and derring-do. For a while we believed all the stories he told us, but I think we loved them—and him—even more after we understood just how tall "tall" was. Two of the most compelling involved equestrian feats. There was the time as a teenager, he told us, when he stood on a horse's bare back as it trotted down the West Market Street hill in Cadiz. Did he really? I certainly couldn't have, but even in old age Grandpa was a vigorous man—so let's say he did. But then there was the time he rode a lion across the ice into St. Petersburg—Russia, not Florida, in case you were wondering. Where was the horse? The horse he was riding, seated this time, was gradually consumed by a pursuing lion until Grandpa was sitting on the lion.

But Grandpa didn't tell stories just to stretch the truth or hear himself talk. It was his way to reach out to us in affection, to delight us and teach us about life. He kept track of all of our accomplishments as we grew up, was proud to bursting of all of us, and like my father after him, made us the protagonists of our own life stories. I couldn't have been more than five on my most memorable early visit to Cadiz, when Grandpa held my hand and Fred's and took us for a walk up the steep Market Street hill to the courthouse. He introduced us to all the Harrison County officials he could find—lawyers, secretaries, reporters, the jailer, the janitor. They all knew that Frank McGavran was in the building that day, and that he had his grandsons Jimmy and Freddy with him. Then he took us upstairs to the attic and let us climb as far as we dared on the wooden ladder that led into the cupola on the roof. From there we could see the town far below us—the post office, the Presbyterian church, and Grandpa's house just across the street from it. And beyond the town, as far as we could see, the grand Eastern Ohio hills ran on under the bright sun. Grandpa gave us that afternoon, that climb, that view, this story—and I still hang onto it for dear life, as I held his hand on those rickety steps so long ago.

I never knew my grandmother except through the rest of the family and what my father told me about her. Her health declined in her fifties: she survived breast cancer but, after suffering for some time from high blood pressure, she died of a massive heart attack the day after Christmas, 1940, just about the time my mother must have begun to wonder whether she was finally pregnant after years of trying. As it turned out, she was—with me—but Grandmother McGavran never knew it. She was beautiful in her youth, to judge from the early photos we have of her, with long, dark hair and big, bright brown eyes; she must also have been a witty, high-energy woman to attract and hold Grandpa's attention. She became a dedicated mother, Dad told me—proud that all five of her children lived through infancy and childhood at a time when many still did not; and she was a strong advocate, ambitious for their success in the world. Like Grandpa, she loved jokes and funny stories, but she had to watch out, because she had a tendency to wet her pants from laughing too hard. She was sentimental too: in one of Dad's essays, he remembered seeing tears stream down her face as she waved goodbye at the railway junction outside of town to some young men going off to fight in World War I. Her early death—she was only sixty—left it up to Grandpa to keep the family together. He remarried two years later, a kind, generous woman who became the only Grandma McGavran that Fred, Molly, and I knew. My father loved Neva and always said that her personality was much like his mother's, but still I came to feel robbed by my blood grandmother's early death. It's partly because, like Dad, I was named for her father, James Holt, another ancestor I never knew, who once looked up at my tall, beautiful mother, winked at Dad, and said, "Big, ain't she?"

Grandpa's older brother, Uncle Doctor, had a personality both magnetic and dictatorial; he could be charming, but he was always firm in his opinions. His wife, Aunt Flora, a renowned beauty in her youth, became one of those delicate, retiring ladies who were always ailing, who quavered rather than spoke—but whose fragility did not prevent her from living close to eighty years. They had lots of money but no children, the opposite of my grandparents on both counts. Trained partly in Germany before World War I, Uncle Doctor performed heroic feats of diagnosis and surgery almost a century before such modern-day medical amenities as MRIs or lasers were available. When Dad was just a teenager, Uncle Doctor saved his life by lancing his pericardium to relieve a buildup of fluid that threatened his heart. With no imaging equipment to guide him, he managed to stick the long needle into Dad's back in exactly the right place and drain the fluid. And when Grandpa's appendix burst, Uncle Doctor saved his life too by successfully performing the appendectomy on the kitchen table in

Cadiz, with the aid of a nurse he brought with him from Columbus, since there was no hospital in Cadiz and Grandpa was too sick to move. In addition to his medical prowess, Uncle Doctor could be very generous, especially with my father, who somehow acquired favorite-nephew status. He and Aunt Flora took Dad on a Mediterranean cruise with them in the late 1920s, and Deje and I still have on our living-room floor one of the Persian rugs they brought back with them.

But they always found ways to remind the rest of the family that they were the ones with the money who did the nice things. Or so it seemed to some of us—which is not to say that simple jealousy of Uncle Doctor's success could be ruled out. In any case, as we were growing up, but especially during and after Aunt Flora's slow decline, my father felt duty-bound to drive across town every Saturday to visit his uncle, regardless of the weather or whatever other weekend tasks he had to do. Fred, Molly, or I often accompanied him on these dreary visits, which even to our young and inexperienced imaginations had acquired the aspect of a royal audience. Mom always enjoyed telling us, especially when she was in one of her "No back talk" moods, that in her youth children were to be "seen but not heard"—but it was worse than that at Uncle Doctor's. We had no choice but to hear his numerous pronouncements with worshipful respect and nod with gratitude whenever he would enlighten us with his opinions. The worst thing of all about Uncle Doctor for getting along in our family—you have probably realized it by now—is that he had no sense of humor. At our gatherings, the rest of us might be howling with laughter while he sat in a corner, grim as death, talking very seriously with whoever he could get to listen—more often than not, my father.

The usurpation of my father's time and the pulling of rank within the family particularly annoyed my mother, who was not intimidated by the money because her own family was wealthy. But since Dad felt truly and deeply obligated to him, Mom had to rein in her urge to tell the old boy off. Put my mother and Uncle Doctor together in the same house and you could count on some sparks flying, if only from Mom's blue eyes. His proven professional skills, combined with his inability to laugh along with his relatives, made the rest of us nervous around him; we deferred to him when we had to speak with him, and tried to avoid him most of the rest of the time. He may have wondered sadly why we didn't chat him up more. But our nervousness had two further results: it made us more error-prone, and it tempted us to deliberate acts of subversion, or at the very least to unholy laughter.

I was jolted back to the present by the arrival of the Manitou boat at the Island ranger station. The rain had held off during the crossing, and it politely waited a little longer still, until we had finished the lunches packed by Deje and Molly early that morning. From that point on until we reached the dunes, the rain would be soft, intermittent, but definitely a part of the hike, although fortunately it didn't always penetrate the tree cover. Far more of a problem were the mosquitoes, the warm-weather nemesis of the North, that deployed themselves in vampire squadrons to feast on us as we passed through the solemn Manitou woods. We had applied insect repellent, but the enemy scorned it. Fred and I wanted to show Molly Lake Florence, snug in its reedy borders, which sits tucked away in the middle of the island, but we could only stop for a moment since even more of the baleful bugs lurked by the still water. Ironically, since they got much worse whenever we stopped walking, they had one beneficial effect: they kept us moving steadily towards our goal.

As we walked on, I returned to my reminiscing. With a chuckle I remembered that Uncle Doctor and Aunt Flora often brought it on themselves. The day I now recalled must have been in the summertime, since Fred, Molly, and I were all at home with Mom, and Dad was at work. We heard a car stopping in the street in front of the house. We looked out and I immediately recognized Uncle Doctor's Lincoln. My mother was surprised and a little irritated when I told her. She had been vacuuming, but the house was not picked up, and she was not dressed for company. Why, uninvited and unexpected, was Uncle Doctor getting out of his car and heading up our sidewalk on a weekday afternoon?

The answer was not immediately clear. Mom opened the door, her fine-lady manners in full display now, while we hid in the living room and tried unsuccessfully to overhear the conversation in the foyer. Uncle Doctor immediately started talking—but somehow not saying much. He said, Mom told us later, that he and Aunt Flora were out for a drive in Upper Arlington, remembered where we lived, and thought they would stop by. But this kind of impromptu social call was unheard of, especially from them. Nor was Mom immediately enlightened when Uncle Doctor returned to the car, opened a rear door, and with great ceremony helped Aunt Flora to get out. He escorted her as she shuffled up the walk to the door, wearing a long black coat in the midst of the summer heat, and it finally dawned on my mother why they had stopped. Aunt Flora needed to relieve herself, she was too feeble to walk up a flight of stairs, and Uncle Doctor remembered that we had a first-floor lavatory near the kitchen. You have to remember that this occurred long before McDonald's and Starbuck's had strewn America with public restrooms.

Mom must have felt some sympathy with Aunt Flora for having endured Uncle Doctor for so many years, but she couldn't help feeling used, and I think she resented his refusal to state his request clearly. She ordered us to stay out of the way while she led Aunt Flora through our dining room to the lavatory. After a considerable while, there came the sound of the toilet flushing, Aunt Flora reappeared smiling, she tottered with Uncle Doctor back down the sidewalk to the Lincoln, and gently he guided her into the back seat again.

We all came out and stood in the front yard to wave them off. We saw Uncle Doctor get in on the driver's side, heard the motor start, and then witnessed a most undignified departure. Instead of gliding forward, the car shot backward along the curb. Uncle Doctor had somehow managed to put the Lincoln into reverse instead of drive. If it had been any other McGavran, we could have imagined it was done intentionally just to give us all a laugh. But Uncle Doctor was incapable of intending to make himself look ridiculous. He stomped on the brake, shifted into drive, and drove away, leaving all of us, including Mom, laughing till our sides hurt. We had great fun telling Dad about it that evening, and we regaled our cousins the next chance we got. If Aunt Flora sustained a whiplash injury, we never heard of it.

Fred, Molly, and I checked our watches and saw we still had plenty of time on the island. So we made a detour before reaching the dunes to see the "Valley of the Giants," one of the few remaining places in the Midwest where old-growth white cedars still stand, somehow passed over by the early lumbermen. In the still, rain-laden air, the huge trunks with their deeply grooved bark rose to the sky as they had done for hundreds of years, towering over a variegated display of wildflowers and ferns. The vertical thrust of the cedar trunks and, beneath them, the fine traceries of colum-bines, trilliums, and jack-in-the-pulpits began to remind me of the

structure and decoration of Gothic cathedrals that I had seen in
England and France: I felt similarly reverent in the vast semi-
enclosed space beneath the dignified old trees. We even found an
altar-like structure of wooden railings, built by the rangers, that
framed and protected the biggest of all the trees, which has since
died and been removed, but was said to be seventeen feet in circum-
ference. It was the perfect place to pause and remember still more
about the family from which we are sprung.

Before I can tell you the funniest Uncle Doctor story of all, I
have to tell you about Thanksgiving. It was the crowning event
in my mother's culinary year. Every November we had
Thanksgiving for all the Columbus McGavrans at our house,
with attendance figures generally hovering between fifteen and
twenty. Starting early in the morning, Mom stuffed and roasted
the giant turkey, prepared mountains of mashed potatoes, and
baked melt-in-the-mouth pies for dessert, while our aunts
brought creamed onions, a green vegetable, a congealed salad, or
perhaps an extra pie. Mom got along well with Dad's sisters, and
like the rest of us, she adored her sister-in-law, my Aunt Mary,
who came from South Georgia and, to our great delight, brought
to all our family events the charming voice and manners of
Scarlett O'Hara at the barbecue. All Aunt Mary had to do was to
show up, and all of us were magically happier; her wit and grit
showed us again and again the very best of what the South had
not lost at the Surrender. While we talked with our cousins in the
living room, the kitchen door might briefly swing open, all the
intoxicating odors of Thanksgiving would waft in upon us, and I
would see my mother at her stove, chatting and laughing with
Aunt Mary as her tall frame swayed over the bubbling pans, a
festive holiday apron tied on to protect a royal blue wool dress
that brought out the blue of her eyes. When the "bird" was done

and had cooled a bit, my father would be summoned to the kitchen to carve the meat, a task he performed with precision and panache that, just as with the washcloth bath ladles, I have never equaled. There were so many of us to feed that as we got older and bigger, the dining-room table wasn't long enough, even with all its leaves, to seat all of us—and so we had to use the breakfast table as well. I remember being truly, deeply happy at those Thanksgiving celebrations so many years ago. What I don't remember, because I only realize it now in the telling, was how hard my mother and aunts worked on those days—partly because they loved doing it, partly for all the rest of us chuckling, bumbling McGavrans, so, in the words of the seasonal hymn, we could "gather together to ask the Lord's blessing"—so we would stay a family bound by both love and duty.

The best Uncle Doctor story occurred during one of these mythic feasts. Aunt Flora was either indisposed or dead by this time, I'm not sure which. Not only was attendance once again near twenty, forcing Mom to set the breakfast table as well as the dining-room table, but there were more of my generation than there were adults, so Mom gave us the dining room and had the adults, including Uncle Doctor, sit in the kitchen. Mom's decision was not intended to deny him his sense of rank; it was just a question of space. Besides, weren't the other grownups also sitting in the kitchen? Still, she and my aunts may have been nervous about putting him there and were trying to make up for it by being especially attentive to him.

In the dining room, Fred, Molly, our cousins, and I had had a great time, as usual, chatting and laughing our way through the huge meal. There was always a lull between dinner and dessert, partly because of the effort involved in clearing away so many dishes, partly because we had all stuffed ourselves so full of turkey, mashed potatoes, and dressing that we welcomed a little time to let those things settle before we went on to eat my mother's pies. We had just been served dessert when my father's younger sister, our sharp-witted, fun-loving Aunt Mary V, swung open the door into the dining room just enough to slip through, and quickly shut the door again. Then she bent over; in fact, she bent double. At first we were alarmed, thinking she must have food poisoning or appendicitis. Then we realized that she was laughing. We immediately demanded to know why, but she was laughing so hard she truly couldn't tell us. Then Aunt Mary arrived in the dining room from the other side, through the living room, tears of laughter literally shooting from her eyes. But it was like laughing in church: they muffled their guffaws so as not to be heard in the kitchen. We were all beside ourselves by now to know what had happened.

When they finally could speak, this was the story they told. Uncle Doctor had chosen pumpkin pie for dessert, and a slice was set before him. Then Aunt Mary V herself had offered him whipped cream. He accepted the offer, and she approached him with a can of Reddi-wip. Yes, even back in the primitive fifties this icon of American dessert gastronomy was widely available. Now whether she held the aerosol can at too acute an angle, or whether my mother's pumpkin pie lacked the requisite surface tension, we will never know. What we do know and will never forget is that my aunt managed to blast gobs of pumpkin pie filling and whipped cream all over Uncle Doctor. It was on his face, his eyeglasses, his shirt and tie—everywhere. Now, as we heard of it, we too were sputtering with suppressed laughter.

Aunts Mary and Mary V finally composed themselves enough to return to the kitchen, but the farce still had another act to play. A few minutes later my father slipped into the dining room, covering his mouth while chuckling as silently as he could, with a follow-up report detailing new depredations upon the august person of our great-uncle. As if trying vicariously to expiate Aunt Mary V's transgression, yet another aunt approached Uncle Doctor with a glass of water and a napkin, thinking to wet the napkin and use it to clean up his face and clothes. Instead she managed to pour the entire glass of water over him, affording him a rinse experience at once more penetrating and less helpful than the one she had planned. We all thought we would explode before we could calm down enough to eat our pie. But we were given stern injunctions by Dad not to come into the kitchen and see the debacle for ourselves; it would humiliate Uncle Doctor to be the object of our stares. So I still laugh when I think about this, not just because it was so funny at the time, but because it brings back so much of the fun of our family gatherings. But I continue also to stifle my laughter because even now I still feel both fear and pity for Uncle Doctor, and I wonder whether he knew what we were thinking and saying about him.

On South Manitou, we doubled back from the cedar grove and regained the forest trail to the western dunes. After a short walk, we passed into a glade of young trees; the crowd of straight, thin young trunks split in two equal groups by the path seemed so ordered, so symmetrical, so calm, that again I felt I was in a holy place. Then the trail abruptly rose, and the rich black soil of the forest floor gave way to soft, steep sand. At first it looked so soft that we feared we would lose our footing in the climb and wear ourselves out thoroughly before we ever saw the big lake or the mainland. But once we started climbing, we found it was no steeper than the main climb at Sleeping Bear. We soon emerged from the forest cover into the open air. It had not only stopped

raining, but the cloudy sky had become bright Leelanau pearlescent. At the same time, a brisk, cool breeze from the big lake
dispersed the mosquitoes and freshened our senses. Now the path
wound upward over the dunes through lush, thick patches of purple, white, and yellow wildflowers. I was delighted to find so
much color where I had not expected it, and amidst the startling
beauty of these remote dunes—recalling my grandparents,
Mom's cooking, Dad's carving, and everything else that happened at our family Thanksgivings—I began to feel healed.

Following the steep trail, we finally came to the moment we
had been waiting for: the high point from which we could look
westward to the big lake, or turn to the southeast and look back
across the island forest and the channel waters all the way to the
mainland at Sleeping Bear Point. Though they still hovered, the
clouds had lifted, and what mist remained in the air didn't spoil, but
subtly enhanced the panorama. Fred, Molly, and I were tired from
our ascent, and at the same time so overwhelmed by the view, that
we said little. As the wind cooled my face and dried out my rain-
soaked T-shirt, I knew South Manitou represented not just a goal
to be reached, but once again, as from the mainland, a symbolic
presentation of alternatives—a geographical means of seeing
choices I had to make about my life, this book, my portrayal of my
parents and the rest of the family. Towards the east now lay the
known world of Leelanau, our present and past lives as I have
attempted to frame them into stories. Towards the west, across the
open lake glowing Delft blue through the haze, lay all that was
unknown and would remain so until I too followed Dad and Mom
and crossed over at my life's end. The breeze off the water spoke of
endless energy, perpetual power, continuous change and renewal;
but the waters themselves looked so deep, so cold, that I knew I
could not swim them and live. Ominously, I saw those waters

through a declivity in the dunes where, as on Sleeping Bear, there was a skeletal mass of long-dead trees, a "ghost forest." Now, with a rush, I realize my struggle to write this book has been like that, like sifting through old broken things to corner spirits—to recapture a past that could never be fully recovered.

A small white butterfly flitted above the bright flowers on the island dunes. I recalled the Monarch in the field by The Ritz that had seemed a spiritual sign, almost a presence, the day of my first return to Leelanau in 2001. But as I write, I remember that two years later, Deje and I had an encounter with butterflies that held both of us spellbound. We were hiking not in Leelanau, but closer to home, in the North Carolina mountains near Mount Mitchell. It was October but still warm, and the leaves were just starting to color. Sunlight shone down, spotlighting a clump of yard-high leafy stalks covered with small, round white blossoms we didn't recognize. We slowed our pace when we noticed that the flowers were practically covered with large and small butterflies of several different species.

Suddenly the two largest, one with yellow and the other with blue wing markings, pulled away from the flowers and faced each other in mid-air. Each seemed to hover and flit around a small invisible sphere that hung between them, separating them. We stared at this aerial pas de deux, at once grotesquely spasmodic and weirdly ethereal. I found myself thinking of the twitchy hologram of Princess Leia in the first *Star Wars* film—"Help me, Obi-Wan-Kenobe, you're my only hope!"—and then of computer-simulated battles of superheroes and their foes in more recent film fantasies like the *Matrix* and *Lord of the Rings* series. But the circling butterflies were real, not virtual. What were they doing? They must not have been mating, since by their markings they were of different species. Nor were they fighting: though they

appeared to collide once or twice, their touching seemed acciden-
tal rather than intentional, for they would immediately separate
and continue their bizarre standoff. We could not figure it out.
The invisible force field that had apparently drawn them together
ceased as suddenly as it had begun. After about a minute, the yellow butterfly veered back to the flowers and resumed feeding,
and the blue followed a few seconds later. They did not feed near
each other, and the blue darted away to another clump of flowers
shortly thereafter. At home a couple of months later, I ran into a
campus colleague of mine, an entomologist, and asked him about
it. He suggested that it was probably not an actual fight, but a
territorial challenge between two males.

But for me it has come to mean more than that: the insects
near the Blue Ridge Parkway visualize for me afresh the tensions
I have felt in Leelanau each time I look at the Manitous. All of my
doubts and questions about my parents and myself, which I have
seen imaged in the islands, dance spasmodically in my brain like
the butterflies. Will the Manitou tensions stop for me as suddenly as the butterflies' dance? Has the long view back across the
island quieted them forever? No: I have another perspective,
that's all—and that's the difference, that's what makes us
human—part of it at least. Questions like mine can never finally
be resolved; we must commit to uncertainty, to contingency. The
butterflies of opposition will go on dancing in my brain, but I
cannot choreograph them.

Fred, Molly, and I started back down the dunes into the still-
dripping South Manitou forest. We had time to catch the boat back
to Leland, but we knew we couldn't dawdle much; besides, those
well-organized mosquitoes charged us again as soon as we reen-
tered the woods. We talked and joked tiredly as we walked: "What

would it really be like to be a mosquito?" "You would be famished, driven, a vampire." "You would always have a buzz on!—heh heh." We were all retiring once more into our personal thoughts.

The next day we went on another, more nostalgic walk: we climbed the Sleeping Bear together again, including the second dune, the one off to the left after the main dune climb, so we could see Little Glen and then, turning around, look far across the dunes and the bright blue water to the Manitous—the view that has haunted me ever since returning to Leelanau. And once again, whenever we fell silent, we relived our individual family memories. For me, now as always, I heard Mom's voice coaching me, and as I climbed with Fred and Molly, my parents' romance and marriage rose into my consciousness.

Mom and Dad met each other at Ohio State in the late 1920s, but apparently no hearts were set ablaze at that time. My mother majored in English, wrote poetry, belonged to Kappa Kappa Gamma sorority, and drove around Columbus in a Ford roadster that she called Pluto—but not in honor of the Disney dog. She had named it instead for a potent laxative of that era, Pluto Water, whose advertising slogan she found congruent with her driving manners: "Pluto Passes Everything!" My father, a member of Sigma Alpha Epsilon, earned a degree in the College of Commerce, but graduating in 1931, in the first, darkest days of the Depression, he didn't find a whole lot of commerce going on. He went to New Jersey for a while, where he got a job in a bank in Montclair. Eventually convinced by the news of the day, but also by his own lack of interest, that banking was not the career for him, he returned to Ohio in 1935 and ran into my mother in downtown Columbus, in the old Woolworth's store on South High Street, across from the "These Are My Jewels" statue of Civil War generals surrounding Mother Ohio on the lawn of the

State Capitol. It was one of the hottest days of a very hot summer—and it was at this time that things began to heat up between them. Dad always used to say that he had met "a million-dollar baby in a five- and ten-cent store"—partly because my mother's family had money, having been landowners in downtown Columbus since the mid-nineteenth century, but mainly, I think, because he was just crazy about her.

Mom was tall, beautiful, clever, and creative. Dad was just an inch taller at five-eleven, with big brown eyes and slicked-back black hair, and he too was both very smart and extremely funny. I think Dad was even better looking than that other Cadiz boy, Clark Gable: Clark's ears were too big. As they got to know each other, Mom and Dad must have had a hell of a good time in spite of the Depression. And it lasted after the honeymoon was over. On a day trip to the Blue Hole in Castalia, Ohio, in the summer of 1937, a year after they were married, they snapped photos of each other that we still have. It was Gable and Rosalind Russell for sure: Mom wore high heels and Dad wore a necktie for a car trip to visit an artesian spring.

We who are middle-aged or older tend to recall our parents closer to the end of their lives than the beginning; we can hardly do otherwise. And in any case, we weren't around to witness their excitement in their first conversations, perhaps shy at first but increasingly eager and more intense; their first dates for movies or ice cream; their long, late-night tellings of their young lives; their falling deeper and deeper in love. Knowing none of this, we still naturally want to imagine that we are living evidence of joyful moments in the long, happy love history of two people. In our case, imagination had it easy. Whatever problems Fred, Molly, and I faced as young people growing up, we didn't have to dream that there was love in our family or wonder where it had disappeared to.

We found powerful further evidence of our parents' love as we were clearing out Mom's last apartment after her death in 2001. It was then we discovered that Dad had written her teasing but passionate love letters all through the summer of 1936, while she attended bridal showers in Columbus and he sold Chevrolets for Grandpa in Cadiz, 120 miles away to the east. He summed up his overwhelming feelings in his last letter, three days before their wedding on September 5:

> Dearest Marion,
>
> Twice in one day I write to you. I must indeed be nuts about you. I know of no other explanation. You know I really do love you very dearly. It's an all mixed up sort of a love—one that makes me want to protect you and at the same time love you to pieces and leave you scattered about the floor. And then there is a very deep love that will go on and on and never be disturbed by any of the more hectic goings-on on the surface. It's a love that may be puzzled and hurt if ever we quarrel but it will continue and will grow and will always be the one thing we can both count on clear down to the end.
>
> . . .
>
> Good night, darling. . . .
>
> > With all my love,
> > Jim

Wanting simultaneously to protect her and literally love her to pieces: even in our X-rated times, Dad's words sizzle. We don't have Mom's letters back to him, but it is not hard to imagine how thrilling such words must have been amid last-minute arrangements with florists and caterers and worries about various relatives' potential for misbehaving. What more could any bride ask for than to have her fiancé describe their feelings as "a love that . . . will continue and will grow and will always be the one thing we can both count on clear down to the end"?

For the wedding, Mom wore an ornately embroidered lace gown that her mother had bought thirty years previously on a trip to Mexico with my grandfather. Because the gown was old-fashioned and elaborately detailed, they posed for their formal wedding pictures in Victorian style, with Dad seated, stiff-backed, and Mom standing behind him in a pose that was somehow both regal and subservient—as if she had just gotten up to fetch him a drink. From earliest childhood, I remember Mom telling us over and over how wonderful love can be between two people, how there really is one Mister or Miss Right for everyone, how we should never sell ourselves short or cheap when picking a life partner. Every day, no matter what she had had to do, she stopped in the late afternoon, showered, and put on a fresh dress or blouse and skirt before Dad came home for dinner. Every evening, when he came in the door, they kissed. Then, before Mom served dinner, they shared their experiences of the day over a Gambrinus beer or a glass of Roma sherry.

They were by no means the last happy McGavran couple. Our daughter Cathy is a physical therapist with a deep concern for her clients and their mobility problems. Drew, equally committed to his work, for several years directed the Erb Institute for Global Sustainable Enterprise at the University of Michigan at Ann Arbor and now has a position as Managing Director for the Graham Environmental Sustainability Institute, also at U of M. They met not at Woolworth's, but at a yoga lesson—their teacher

Christy was a wedding guest. Their feelings for each other gradually grew deeper, much as I think my parents' love had done
some seventy years earlier, and as Deje's and my attachment took
off in the late 1960s after an earlier period of knowing each other
as part of a larger group of friends at the College of William and
Mary, where we both were English instructors. It was clear to us
from our first meeting with him that Drew is a brilliant and
charming young man, and that Cathy glowed whenever he was
around. Drew later got high marks from Cathy's brothers Mark
and Jamie, who like Deje and me could not help liking him or
noticing the sparkle in their sister's eyes. I had misplaced my
father's love letters to Mom or I would have asked to read at the
wedding from the one I quoted earlier; but it was unnecessary,
since if two people ever were in possession of a "very deep love"
that they could count on, it's Cathy and Drew.

Once Deje and I started our annual returns to Leelanau, we
asked them to visit us in the house at Cedar. They immediately
responded to the beauty of the place: the lakeshore, orchards, and
forests that I knew from childhood and that Deje now enjoys with
me. We hiked the dunes, the Alligator, Pyramid Point, and Cathead
Bay together. In addition Drew, a dedicated golfer and native
Michigander, began renewing his acquaintance with courses in the
area. So after they became engaged, it must have seemed almost a
no-brainer for them to decide to have the wedding in Leelanau.

After searching around the peninsula, they found the
Vineyard Inn, just north of the center of Suttons Bay. The rooms
in this small hotel look east over a descending lawn to a narrow
beach and a dock on the bay. A big red maple halfway between the
building and the lake stands out against the brightness of the
water behind it and provided a perfect focal point for the wedding
ceremony. The June weather was cool and invigorating, and the

sky that day shone with the same bright pearlescent glow I have come to recognize and love from many of our hikes.

The night before the wedding, Drew's parents, Sally and Vince Horning, invited a large crowd of us to dinner at the Café Bliss in Suttons Bay. I would call this the rehearsal dinner, but Drew and Cathy had planned their wedding so carefully that no rehearsal was necessary, just a couple of conversations with Diane Mowrey, a Presbyterian minister and Deje's colleague at Queens University of Charlotte, who flew north to officiate at the wedding. The only music during the wedding itself was played by John Wunsch, a guitarist from Interlochen Music College. But before we went to Café Bliss the night before, Mark and I played music at the Vineyard, where most of the guests stayed, on instruments that our friends Bill and Dorothy Roberts brought in the back of their car all the way from Charlotte—Mark's acoustic guitar and a keyboard for me to use to play duets with him. Mark was already into Django Reinhardt, so we had learned "See You in My Dreams" and "Limehouse Blues," two numbers that my father could easily have played along with, and a couple of Beatles tunes as well.

Diane, Cathy, and Drew put together a powerful wedding service that mixed Christian liturgy and prayers with Native American traditions of respect for the elements of nature and a sense of oneness with all the earth, a sense of belonging in space and time. It was as if Mishimokwa, the Sleeping Bear of Ojibwa legend, had awakened in hope from her deep, despairing slumbers and found a human voice. A paragraph from Diane's homily summarizes this eloquently:

> As you build your new life together, remember also to listen
> to the heartbeat, the soul, of the natural world around you.

For there is indeed a force that drives the flower, the hills, the water, and the wind—and that drives us. That force—at the heart of the universe—is a heart, and its lifeblood is love. Root your love, then, in this deeper, divine love.

Fred and Liz and Molly and John and their families were there, and I kept thinking how happy my parents would have been to witness this service that celebrated not just the wedding, but a revival of our family's tradition of returning year after year to Leelanau. Perhaps, somehow, they were there.

As emotional as I usually am at formal celebrations, I was so happy at this wedding that I pretty much managed not to cry. Drew's two nieces Katie and Anna Horning, and Eva Roth, the daughter of Cathy's Kenyon friend Julie Roth and her husband Randy, served charmingly as flower girls. The photos our Charlotte friend Sharon Frazier took of them, of Jamie and Mark escorting Deje to her seat in front of all the assembled guests, and of Cathy and me walking out to meet Drew and Diane, show all of us laughing with elation. No wonder, really: I was escorting the most beautiful bride (but one) that I had ever seen, and I couldn't feel sad. I wanted to live entirely in that moment so I would always have it with me in my heart. Cathy wore a simple short white linen dress, tie-up cork-heeled sandals from Spain that Beth Ostrowski, her childhood friend from Charlotte, had found for her, and a ring of fresh flowers in her long blond hair. She also carried a family heirloom: an old lace handkerchief that Deje had found buried in a dresser drawer earlier that spring, one that both my mother and Molly had carried in their weddings.

My only close calls with tears occurred first when I looked back over the guests and saw them in Beth's and Julie's eyes, and later when during the ceremony Diane read some beautiful words about Cathy:

We are grateful for Catherine's devotion to family and friends, for her dedication to caring and helping others, and her ability to respect the needs of others and to tolerate the quirkiness of humanity. We give thanks for her child-like playfulness, her infectious smile and her joyful laugh, and we are all inspired by her respect for all of life.

After the ceremony, Diane told us that she had asked Drew and Cathy to tell her some of the things that each loved or admired about the other—and this was Drew's list. Realizing that he knew and treasured so many of the same things about her that we do, Deje and I felt the great joy of knowing that our daughter would always be loved and respected in her marriage.

After the ceremony, a buffet dinner catered by the excellent (but sadly now defunct) Café Bliss was served under a big white tent on the lawn of the Inn, which itself was resplendent with summer flowers in beds, pots, and hanging baskets. On each table were fresh flowers picked that same morning at Omena Flowers, a U-Pick florist just four miles up the road from the Inn, by Cathy, Deje, Molly, Sally, Katie, Anna, and many of the other women attending the wedding. Also gracing each table were a few of the heart-shaped Lake Michigan stones we had been collecting since the previous summer.

Deje had suggested just that morning that I should prepare some remarks to be given as a toast for the new bride and groom. This threw me at first, not only because I was afraid I would lose my composure, but also because I wasn't sure what to say. Deje offered some great suggestions—in fact what I ended up with is as least as much hers as mine—but as the moment approached I was still very nervous about getting choked up. Fortunately, McGavranesque absurdity intervened at the last minute to banish pomposity and keep me laughing. In a comeuppance as symbolic as the Thanksgiving disaster that dumped pumpkin pie all over Uncle Doctor many years earlier, my suit jacket, and thus my rear end, got stuck in the folding chair I was sitting in and I literally could not stand up to read my remarks until my brand-new son-in-law Drew, who was sitting next to me, managed to extricate me. We all were laughing so hard at this turn of events that it was impossible to cry. This is what I said:

> Cathy's first word was not "Mama," nor "Dada," but "Happy." She would lie in her crib, gurgling and saying "Happy happy happy." She was the very image of innocent joy and beauty—our first child and, as it turned out, our only daughter. As a preschooler, she amazed us with a painting of a caterpillar turning into a butterfly—not a caterpillar, and not a butterfly, but the metamorphosis. A few years later she regaled us with the tragedy of the typewriter who fell in love with a pizza: "He loved her but she was *gone.*"
>
> Her life has brought many metamorphoses since then: dancer, student, skilled professional. And ever since she met Drew at Christy's yoga class, love has brought her a happiness as joyous as that of her girlhood, but far deeper. We have never seen Catherine as happy as she is now. So my toast to you both is—live happy, never stop the process, the dance, the forward motion, the love that is in your hearts.

After that, we all laughed and talked and danced under the tent while the twilight deepened and the dark waters of Leelanau played the sweetest, gentlest imaginable marriage song on the beach below.

PART FIVE

HOMECOMING

It's July 2007, Deje and I are back in Leelanau, and the Monarchs have taken over. We've never seen so many. They dart over the sidewalks when we shop in town, over the dunes when we go hiking, over the beaches on hot afternoons. Again and again one dances right up to our eyes, hovers an instant, then flies off. I pull out my digital camera and try to catch them in my pixel net—but they hardly ever alight. What are they up to? When do they eat? They don't seem to be mating, yet they almost seem driven. Can they too be spectral butterflies, carriers again of the spirits of my parents? Fred wrote a prize-winning short story several years ago whose main character believed that butterflies were rents in the veil of everyday life, and their gorgeous wings revealed the colors of heaven. Now, however, after years of chasing ghosts, spiritual uncertainty gives way to physical delight, and I simply enjoy the show these long-distance migrants put on.

If the Monarchs bring me particular joy, it is another itinerant species that pleases Deje: the knapweed flowers that cast their rose-lavender tint over the meadows and dunes of Leelanau every July. This year they too seem particularly abundant. When for the first time we hike the Bayview Trail with Cathy and Drew, we see them again and again, perfectly arranged with fields, shrubs, small trees, and sometimes distant waters in Monet-like Impressionist compositions. Deje is thrilled—we all are, actually—and since the flowers can't fly away but only bend in the breeze, I take shot after shot with the digital. Then Cathy remarks that knapweed is not native to Michigan, that in fact it has invaded the state. This surprises us—the flowers do seem to "belong" here. But she has to be right; we know that she and Drew studied Michigan native plants extensively while planning their garden in Ann Arbor. Most of us fail to realize how much botanical life, just like animal and human life, is for one reason or another migratory. How did knapweed come to Leelanau? Were the seeds blown by the wind, or did they stick to the wheels of cars or trucks? Did Lakeshore personnel start planting them after the 1970 takeover to help stabilize the dunes? Probably not, for I have since learned that knapweed is slowly crowding out the milkweed the Monarchs need to lay their eggs on. In any case the Monarchs flit among the blooms, and Deje loves them.

Still other imported species truly dominate life in Leelanau in July. Tourists and locals, everyone asks about the cherries: "Was there another late frost like in '02?" "How does the crop look this year?" "Will the farmers make anything?" But community concern eventually gives way to individual desire, and the question becomes, "Have you seen sweet cherries at the roadside stands yet?" Unless it is a very bad year, the cherries take over the landscape. Orchards are visible from nearly every road in the county. The rows of low, gnarled trees remind me of similar neat rows of olive trees curving up the high, rolling hills of Tuscany—partly because many cherry farmers also plant rows of Lombardy poplars from Italy as windbreaks. And as with the Tuscan olive groves, Leelanau's cherry orchards increasingly alternate with vineyards as more Michigan farmers grow grapes for winemaking. But it is the cherry trees' moment in the sun, literally and figuratively, and they make the most of it. As it ripens, the fruit weighs down the twisted branches, sometimes cracking one till it falls to the ground. And everywhere they incarnate the summer sun, casting their blood-red glow over the fields and hills.

The house we rent lies surrounded by orchards in a wooded residential area between Cedar and Good Harbor Bay. Just past the house, there's a break in the woods where the road dead-ends, and the cherry trees in their neat rows stand right up to the barrier. If I look up from my book while reading on the front deck, I can see their leaves dancing in the breeze even though the branches sag with the weight of the fruit. At night we see cherries in our headlights when we return after watching the sun set into the bay. To be sure, we often see deer in the orchards, day and night, while crows and gulls hover above and wild turkeys waddle among the rows; one evening we even saw a family of skunks prancing up Good Harbor Trail. Still, in July, in spite of these animal distractions, the cherries take and hold center stage.

Once the picking begins, we wake up early to the dull but steady groans of the "shakers"—harvesting machines that shake the trees to make the fruit fall. Ordinarily, this kind of noise at any time of day sends us both up the wall. At home in Charlotte we complain about the sounds of construction and renovation in our inner-city neighborhood, and I have an almost irrational loathing of the whine of the leaf blowers that shatter our weekend peace for about two months every fall. But when we're Up North, we don't mind it when the shakers' droning enters at the kitchen door and mingles with the cheerful gurgle of the coffee maker.

The reason is simple: it makes us city slickers from the New South feel connected, however indirectly, to the earth and sky of Leelanau. To be sure, there is a wide variety of agricultural production in the county, and more and more of the cherry farmers have diversified into other fruits—apples and peaches as well as grapes—and field crops as well, especially since that late-frost disaster in 2002. True, also, that both fields and orchards are yielding more and more in recent years to the developers' backhoes. But it's the cherries that have laid hold of my imagination since childhood. Other vacationers must feel the same, to judge from the success of the Cherry Republic in marketing Northland edibles and nostalgia—a process in which we participate by shopping the store in Glen Arbor and by online ordering of holiday packages. But most of our Leelanau cherry dollars go into the trust boxes at roadside stands all over the peninsula where growers leave quarts of the delicious just-picked fruit for passersby to purchase. Sadly, in recent years local farmers have had their trust boxes broken into and the money stolen.

For me, there's more to it than the flavor of the fruit. The orchards prove that nature and human industry can combine in a measured, ordered beauty that contrasts with, yet perfectly complements the wild, random forms of the dunes, the forests, and the lakeshore. Backed by the tall, trembling columns of poplars, the neat rows of low-arcing trunks offer me a pattern of grace. As with the ancient cedars on South Manitou, the cherry trees become arches and pillars in an open-air cathedral, as stately and solemn in their way as Salisbury or Chartres, yet closer to and more intimate with this Michigan land that we love. The contorted or broken shapes of the branches, like the statues of saints and martyrs in the cathedrals, hint at the pain and suffering that must inevitably accompany the dignity and order of life. As a summer visitor, I have never seen the orchards in blossom time, with their lighter-than-snow beauty and promise for the future. But the harvest, when entire hillsides glow crimson in the sunlight, radiates an irresistible splendor of abundance, color, and life. It's the moment of fulfillment before the inevitable darkening into winter and death. I am always glad to be a July visitor.

Since they have appeared on the Leelanau landscape for only about a century, the orchards offer not just their churchly dignity, but another reminder of the transitory inhabitants and livelihoods to appear over time in this remote part of Lower Michigan. Many populations have come, and then either gone, or stayed, or returned. First were the Odawas and Ojibwas, the tribes who seasonally entered and departed the forests and shores, and whose descendants live at Peshawbestown, just north of Suttons Bay. Then came the mostly French fur trappers, the first whites to arrive, and following them in the nineteenth century the mostly Anglo, Norwegian, and Central European workers in the lumber camps. By the latter part of the nineteenth century, the farmers, business people, and teachers had started coming—along with the tourists like me, who have been arriving, departing, and returning for at least a century and a quarter, and the Mexican pickers who first came to Leelanau in the 1920s, as if following the Monarchs out of Yucatán.

Some of this history of immigration can be traced in the area immediately adjacent to our rented house in Cedar. After we turn north onto M-22 from Town Line Road to go for groceries at the Leland Mercantile, we immediately pass St. Luke's Lutheran Church, a landmark important to another, earlier era when, like the Mexican pickers, other foreign-born people came to work and earn a livelihood. During the latter half of the nineteenth century, when land had to be cleared before it could be farmed, the Good Harbor Bay area saw the rapid rise and fall of two active lumber towns. The church, rebuilt and expanded after 1919, had its origins in the village of Good Harbor, first established in 1863 around the

Schomberg Lumber Company. Here were once eighteen houses, two general stores, a post office, a boarding house, a feed barn, and a saloon. Now historians refer to it as a ghost town, but there is nothing left to see, ghostly or otherwise, except the church and its graveyard and the remains of a loading dock down on the beach. After the lumber mill burned down in 1906, when nearly all the original timber had already been cut and sold, inhabitants began to move away. But this was not the first town of its type on the bay. Bohemian immigrants had sailed north from Chicago back in the mid-1850s and started a town they called North Unity a little west of Good Harbor village. As with the later settlement, there were houses, a store, and a post office; in a second and more sinister parallel, this population too began to leave after a disastrous fire—this one occurring in 1871. Visitors to the area now can see none of this, but a drive to the Port Oneida community, on the Glen Arbor side of Pyramid Point, or to Glen Haven, where both restoration and "old" new construction has taken place, gives something of the feel of what these small coastal communities must have been like. Private as well as Lakeshore money often is invested in historic preservation: in the summer of 2004, at least one old barn was being dismantled piece by piece and moved by its owner across the county to a new location.

Good Harbor Bay today is one of the most beautiful and heavily used beaches along Leelanau's shores. Kayakers paddle on the lake, swimmers and sunbathers abound, and on a hot afternoon we will add to their number. After we've swum, we often feel like going for a walk, so Deje and I will begin trudging west around the curving shoreline towards Pyramid Point, or east towards the Whaleback until the "Private Property" signs remind us that the residents with shore frontage between here and Leland do not like to share their view with strangers. In spite of posted restrictions, dog owners either walk their dogs along the shore or let them run about, leaping and splashing in and out of the big lake and then vigorously shaking themselves dry, as our dear old Mickey did after swimming in Little Glen half a century ago. Many beach visitors bring materials for a cookout and stay on into the evening, toasting s'mores, drinking beer, and hoping for a glorious sunset. And often they are not disappointed; in July the sun sinks right between the North and South Manitou Islands—sometimes in a great pale aqua sky filled with coral, gold, and purple clouds; sometimes with a perfectly clear upper sky and just a low streak of gray cloud, close down to the water, through which the last rays will break out suddenly in brilliant copper-orange streaks. Charcoal bits, charred logs, beverage cans, and plastic trash often clutter up this perhaps too-popular beach; and sadly, eco-trash lines the shore of the big lake itself. Whenever we swim, we must wade through the green algae that piles up both in and out of the water; then, just inside the water's edge, we must step carefully to avoid the zebra mussel shells that cause the algae's growth. With pollution accumulating both on the sand and in the water, it may seem strange that so many people return year after year. But visitors and locals alike love Good Harbor, and there is as yet no decline in tourism to parallel those in lumbering and farming.

Rural life has become more difficult for family farmers in Leelanau. They've battled harsh weather, fluctuating prices, and vacation developers for generations, and now, like their counterparts all over the country, they find it harder and harder to make a sufficient profit in the face of concerns about global climate change, and steadily mounting growing and harvesting costs that favor larger landowners—agribusinesses—over smaller family acreages. The disastrous cherry crop failure in Leelanau in

2002 cut overall farm production almost in half and raised government payments to farmers by 645% for the period 1997–2002.
The same costs make it even more difficult for those who would
like to begin farming careers, whether by buying an existing
farm or starting a new one; now, however, some farming hopefuls
are leasing land and equipment from established growers in
order to get started. Still, in spite of all these setbacks, Leelanau
continues to produce more tart cherries than any other single
county in the United States.

We feel connected to Leelanau farmers through a family we do
not know, but about whom we have read with interest and concern.
Whenever we leave the house in the orchard, we exit onto Eitzen
Road and then, most days, take Town Line Road up, over, and down
a long hill that gives a beautiful view of Good Harbor Bay from the
top. At the bottom of the hill, just before Town Line dead-ends into
M-22 at the Lutheran church, we always notice the small white
farmhouse, over a century old now, where four generations of the
Eitzen family lived and worked, raising dairy cows, chickens, potatoes, field crops—and cherries. We felt we got to know them, in fact
our hearts went out to them, when we read about them in the
Leelanau Enterprise and learned how, like many other local landowners in the 1970s, the Eitzens agreed under pressure to sign
their property over to the Sleeping Bear National Lakeshore. Their
twenty-five-year lease with the Lakeshore expired on the Fourth of
July, 2003—an ironic date to say the least, since in many ways,
though they still own land outside the park boundary, they lost at
least some of their sense of freedom to control their lives. The head
of the family since her husband Lloyd died, Virginia Eitzen had
made her home on the farm for fifty years since she came as a young
bride from Flint. As the family moved out, she commented, with
painful understatement, "It feels like a funeral. . . . It's the end of

something." It doesn't take a year-round Leelanau address to feel and sympathize with what was in Mrs. Eitzen's mind at that moment: the years and years of planting, cultivating, harvesting the good crops and the bad crops; not just the bright July day of their final farewell to the farm, but all the fierce late-autumn storms, the icy Januaries, the messy spring thaws, the blossoms, and then the anxious waiting to see if time and weather are favorable for yet another year's crop. Their only real consolation at this partly agreed-on, partly coerced departure—and it is an important one— was that the Lakeshore officials had agreed to leave the old house standing, as they have done with some homes in the Port Oneida community and elsewhere, as a memorial to the consecrated rural life the family shared there for so long. Recognizing the power of the Lakeshore to maintain as well as sweep aside, Mrs. Eitzen commented wryly, "The only good thing about it is, someday down the road, you won't see a cluster of houses here; it will be preserved." It seems that although she didn't exactly have a choice in the matter, she was relieved that between the Lakeshore feds and the real-estate developers, it was the feds who won, because they would keep the memory of the family alive. All this goes through our minds each time we drive by the old white farmhouse at the bottom of the Town Line hill.

The cherry stand on Good Harbor Trail, just south of the Eitzen Road turnoff, is the prettiest one we have seen in Leelanau. Brightly painted white, with big red-and-white illustrated signs, it has tempted us to stop every year since we first began staying in the area. As we approach for the first time this year, we are happy to see a sign on the opposite side of the road pointing to the shed and saying, "Open." We stop and see that there are several quarts of fresh-picked sweet cherries. I get out of the car and put our three dollars into the locked cash box before I notice a small note written in a fine feminine hand. The note explains apologetically that buyers must have exact change since it is no longer possible to trust passersby not to steal from the change fund. It's signed "Virginia Eitzen." Now Deje and I are even more pleased; it has already been four years since the Eitzens' story was in the *Enterprise*, but now for the first time we know it is their stand, and we feel able to connect with them, however indirectly, by purchasing and eating their produce.

Of course the cherries are fabulous, and we stop back at the stand regularly during our two-week stay to buy more. The day before we leave, I make one last stop there, so we can take fresh cherries to Cathy and Drew down in Ann Arbor. As I stop the car, I see that there is just one quart of cherries sitting on the table. Lucky me, I think; those are "my" cherries. I start to slide my three dollars into the slot when a white Chevrolet wagon pulls up, and I think I will have to explain to the driver that I have just bought the last of the cherries. Instead, a voice calls out from the car, "Wait, I have some new cherries we just picked. You should take one of these." When I look, I see a tall, graceful woman with white hair and beautiful clear eyes. In her arms she holds several quarts of fresh cherries. I know who it has to be—and who I want it to be—but I ask her to make sure: "Are you Mrs. Eitzen?" She says yes, and immediately I start jabbering like a shy schoolboy trying to chat up the homecoming queen. I tell her how beautiful her family's orchards are, how much we enjoy living nearby, how moved we were to read of her family's experience in the newspaper four years previously. She asks politely where we come from and where we stay. We talk for a minute more, and it is only after she says she is glad to meet me and drives off that I realize I haven't even told her my name.

I feel both exhilarated and foolish. I was so excited I had almost forgotten to breathe. I stay for a moment by the cherry stand; then I speed down Eitzen Road to tell Deje. But what could I tell her, beyond the fact of it? What exactly has happened? I wasn't sure that day, or for some time thereafter. But now, as I write about it, I know that I have made a new connection with the place I have written so much about. No, that's not right; a connection has been made for me. By arriving at that moment and offering fresh cherries, Mrs. Eitzen made it possible for me to feel more fully a part of Leelanau than I ever had before, as boy or man. Now I think my earlier simile was strangely apt: in that moment of simple kindness, she actually became the queen of the county; she presided over my "homecoming" into Leelanau and blessed it. She gave me the welcome I had longed for ever since I first returned, after the death of my parents. And she wasn't a ghost; she was real.

SOURCES

PART ONE. THE WAY BACK

Anne-Marie Oomen, *Seasons of the Sleeping Bear* (1999).

Henry David Thoreau, *The Illustrated Walden*, edited by J. Lyndon Shanley (Princeton: Princeton University Press, 1973).

Ruth Young, letter to the author, 31 January 2005.

PART TWO. SHADOWING MOM

Eric Carlson, "Cougar Verified in Lakeshore . . ." *Leelanau Enterprise*, 23 January 2003; a later article by Carlson, "6-month Study: No Evidence of Cougars," on 16 February 2006, declared that after more study there was no evidence of cougars in the Lakeshore.

Harry R. Dumbrille, "The Sleeping Bear," "Sleeping Bear Pinnacle," quoted in George Weeks, *Sleeping Bear: Yesterday and Today* (Franklin, MI: Altwerger and Mandel, 1990).

Frank C. Gates, "The Disappearing Sleeping Bear Dune," *Ecology* 31 (1950): 386–92.

Theodore J. Karamanski, *A Nationalized Lakeshore*, www.Leelanau.com, June 2003.

Anne-Marie Oomen, "Alone on the Winter Dune," *Traverse* (February 2003).

Sleeping Bear Dunes National Lakeshore, brochure (National Park Service, 1989).

Kathleen Stocking, *Letters from the Leelanau: Essays of People and Place* (Ann Arbor: University of Michigan Press, 1990).

Tom Ulrich, SBNL assistant superintendent, interview with author, July 2003.

149

George Weeks, *Sleeping Bear: Yesterday and Today* (Franklin, MI: Altwerger and Mandel, 1990).

Steve Yancho, Lakeshore ranger, interview with author, July 2003.

PART THREE. SHADOWS OF DAD

Elna Greenan Garthe and Sue Woodward, interview with author, July 2003.

Jack and Ruth Lambkin, interview with author, July 2003.

PART FIVE. HOMECOMING

Eric Carlson, "Census of Agriculture," *Leelanau Enterprise*, 15 July 2004.

Sarah Chapman, "Young Farmers Find It Difficult," *Leelanau Enterprise*, 1 July 2004.

Susan Olsen Haswell and Arnold R. Alanen, *A Garden Apart: An Agricultural and Settlement History of Michigan's Sleeping Bear Dunes National Lakeshore Region* (Omaha, NE: National Park Service, 1994).

Amy Hubbell, "Letting Go of the Eitzen Family Farm," *Leelanau Enterprise*, 10 July 2003.

————"Thieves Hitting Produce Stand," *Leelanau Enterprise*, 12 August 2004.

George Weeks, *Sleeping Bear: Yesterday and Today* (on North Unity and Good Harbor settlements) (Franklin, MI: Altwerger and Mandel, 1990).

Gitta Laasby, "Cherry Answers Sought," *Leelanau Enterprise*, 3 June 2004.

ACKNOWLEDGMENTS

First I must thank my brother and sister, Fred McGavran and Molly Crabb, for their help and encouragement throughout the seven years that this book has taken to complete. They have returned again and again to Leelanau with Deje and me, and have been our steady companions on the trails and the beaches, altering some of my memories and adding others of their own. They do not agree with all facets of my portrayal of our parents and our early lives, but they have been generous in agreeing that ultimately this had to be my version of the story. I also thank my sister-in-law Liz McGavran and my brother-in-law John Crabb for putting up with so much McGavraniana for so long.

The University of North Carolina at Charlotte awarded me a Summer Research Grant in 2003 that supported my first explorations in Leelanau. Thanks to that funding, I was able to interview Leelanau writers Anne-Marie Oomen and Kathleen Stocking, Good Harbor Grill owner Brendan Burrows, longtime Little Glen residents Elna Greenan Garthe and Sue Woodward, longtime Empire residents Jack and Ruth Lambkin, David Taghon of the Empire Museum, Homestead president Bob Kuras, and George Weeks, historian of the Sleeping Bear. I am grateful to all of them, and for additional interviews that summer with several Sleeping Bear National Lakeshore professionals: assistant superintendent Tom Ulrich, rangers Steve Yancho and Max

Holden (now retired), and trail designer Leigh Evans. Special thanks for her early and continuing encouragement are due to Barbara Siepker, owner of the Cottage Bookshop in Glen Arbor. I am also indebted to Laura Quackenbush, curator of the Leelanau Historical Museum in Leland, for sharing her knowledge of the region and for allowing me access to many materials relating to the history of Leelanau, its peoples, and its tourist industry. Thanks as well to Jim and Karen Ladd, our Leelanau landlords, for our annual returns since 2002 to their lovely home near Good Harbor Bay.

As an English professor, I have published many an academic article and book chapter. But this was my first attempt at creative writing, and it would never have succeeded without the help of many people over the years. Our Outer Banks friend Jan De Blieu read an early version of the first chapter and realized, I hope, in spite of its roughness, how indebted I was and still am to her brilliant 1994 *Orion* essay "Mapping the Sacred Places." My former UNC Charlotte English Department colleague Sam Watson, now retired, must have despaired of it, it took so long, but he finally got me to see that even though I was a Wordsworth scholar writing a very Wordsworthian memoir, I needn't feel compelled to quote the great British poet of nature and memory every third page. Later, another colleague, fiction writer Aimee Parkison, read the manuscript, annotating every page with notes and suggestions that greatly strengthened both its structure and expression. Most recently, still another colleague and longtime friend, novelist and poet Karon Luddy, decorated the entire manuscript with insightful comments that led me to a final, transforming revision.

I thank the editorial staff of the Michigan State University Press, especially Acquisitions Editor Martha Bates, without whose interest and support *In the Shadow of the Bear* would have remained in the shadows.

The whole project would never have been possible without the constant encouragement and sharp-eyed commentaries of my beautiful, brilliant, long-suffering wife Deje, who loves Leelanau as I do and always made it easier for me to work on the book. Our beloved children Catherine, Mark, and Jamie, and Cathy's husband Drew Horning all have helped me more than they know with their enthusiasm for the project. The dedication expresses my greatest debt of all—the debt for which I hope this book offers some small measure of repayment.